Heaven's Reality: Lifting the Quantum Veil

Dr. Sarah A. McGee

Heaven's Reality: Lifting the Quantum Veil
Copyright © 2016 Sarah McGee

ISBN: 978-0-9977309-0-6

All rights reserved. No part of this book may be reproduced or transmitted in any form or by any means without written permission from the author.

All Scripture quotations, unless otherwise indicated, are taken from the Holy Bible, New International Version®, NIV®. Copyright ©1973, 1978, 1984, 2011 by Biblica, Inc.™ Used by permission of Zondervan. All rights reserved worldwide. www.zondervan.com

Scripture quotations marked (ESV) are from The Holy Bible, English Standard Version® (ESV®), copyright © 2001 by Crossway, a publishing ministry of Good News Publishers. Used by permission. All rights reserved.

Scripture quotations marked (NASB) are taken from the New American Standard Bible®, Copyright © 1960, 1962, 1963, 1968, 1971, 1972, 1973, 1975, 1977, 1995 by The Lockman Foundation. Used by permission. (www.Lockman.org)

Printed in America
Glistening Prospect Bookhouse
GlisteningProspectBookhouse.com

To the Glory of God

Table of Contents

Chapter 0: Introduction 1

Chapter 1: The Substance of Reality 15

Chapter 2: Higher Dimensional Space 49

Chapter 3: Time & Eternity 69

Chapter 4: Quantum Leaping 83

Chapter 5: Quantum Unity 101

Chapter 6: Quantum Observation 113

Chapter 7: Q & A 135

Chapter 8: Conclusion 149

Chapter 0
Introduction

I grew up in a home that strongly valued understanding God and Science. My parents were always ministering to the poor and leading Bible studies in our home. We were always talking about God and His ways. And, we saw Him working mightily in our family and in those my parents were ministering to.

My parents constantly emphasized applying the lessons God was teaching us through His Word to our own lives and in ministry to help others. We got to see how well we understood God's principles of love and life as we saw them working in our lives and in those we were ministering to. Then, we could go back to God and get deeper and better understanding when something wasn't working so well.

So, I guess you could say that I grew up in a family that valued "research theology." We didn't just want to study the Scriptures and find out what we believed that they said, or simply take some preacher or scholar's word for what the Bible said. We wanted to know what actually works and what is actually real and true based on the evidence of people's changed lives. We always wanted to go deeper and deeper into knowing God and His character and nature. We wanted to know what God is truly like and how He works, not just what people said He was like.

My family was also very big into science and wanting to understand everything about how the world works. My dad started out as a Nuclear Engineer and then did many other things before ending up in full time ministry. He is constantly thinking about the big picture and about how every piece fits together and affects each other. He is wired to look at the science behind everything, both in the details and in the big picture as well as in all their interactions.

My father is also an amazing teacher and storyteller. My parents were always teaching us about how the world works in every circumstance. When we were little, we would ask all the "why, why, why" questions. However, unlike most kids, we never got a chance to ask the second "why" because Dad would go on for four hours about more than you would ever want to know in answer to the first "why" question. But, he made sure to explain it in little kid terms so we could understand it.

Take, for example, the common question, "Why are the leaves green?" First off, Dad would say, "Well, what is green?" Because we have to understand what our assumptions and starting place is in order to answer the question properly. So, Dad would pull out a prism and show us the rainbow. Then, he would explain how light from the sun is really made out of all these different colors, and one of them is defined as green. That is what green is.

Now that we have a starting place, Dad would then get a leaf and show it to us. He would break the leaf and show us the little boxes on the ragged edge. He would explain that each of those little boxes are called "cells" and that there are lots of different types of cells that make up all the different parts of the plant and we are made out of cells too.

Inside the plant cells, there are tiny things that absorb the sunlight and turn it into food for the plant to live and grow. It is kind of like a little power generator that uses light for fuel. The power generators inside the cell actually don't need much of the green light, so they reflect it and send it back out of the leaf. That is why the leaves look green to us. But, we can't stop there. We always need to dig deeper.

The little power generators also need carbon dioxide to make the conversion from sunlight to energy work. Carbon dioxide is what we and all the other animals breathe out because we have too much of it, but the plants love it and need it. After they use up the carbon dioxide, the plants have a lot of oxygen left over which they can't use. So, the plants release the excess oxygen into the air. Conveniently, we need to breathe in the oxygen in the air to live. We would die if we didn't keep breathing in oxygen. The little power generators in the cells in the leaves give out green light and oxygen while they are making food for the plant.

Then, Dad would explain how the plant absorbs the sunlight and carbon dioxide and turns them into food energy for the plant. That makes the plants grow and makes fruit, seeds, and all the other parts of the plant. Then, we eat the fruit, seeds, and leaves to give us energy to live and grow. All the other animals do too. All the energy we need to live and grow comes from the plants, which comes from the sun. So, God made the leaves green so we could have food to eat and air to breathe. God loves us and He designed everything to take care of us and work together with us.

Dad would be constantly explaining how everything works from the beginning to the end and explaining how everything interacts and affects everything else. And, he would continually relate everything to God and His love for us.

So, I grew up with a love for God and a love for science. I want to know God and His ways more and more. I also desire to understand how brilliantly God made the universe in all of its intricacies. I long to understand how everything works and understand how everything works together. I've always been drawn to learning the simple principles that govern the incredibly complicated behavior of all the matter in the universe.

I decided to get a Ph.D. in theoretical quantum physics so I could learn more about the building blocks of the universe and the science of the non-physical realm. Quantum physics studies tiny sub-atomic particles, which are the building blocks of all the matter and light in the universe. Science has discovered that quantum particles are not entirely physical. Even though this is quite confusing to many scientists and non-scientists alike, we have still discovered many intriguing laws and principles about how these not quite physical particles work. I will explain more about that in detail in the next chapter and throughout this book.

In my studies, I have also learned quite a bit about what science has to say about God. What God said in the Bible about His creation revealing His power and nature is true.

> *Romans 1:20, "For since the creation of the world God's invisible qualities--his eternal power and divine nature--have been clearly seen, being understood from what has been made, so that people are without excuse."*

There are many truths about God that science has discovered and corroborated. However, there are certainly many cases where the scientists don't really realize that they have discovered something about God. Never the less, studying creation can only point to the creator. God has hidden truths about Himself in nature for us to find. I found many of these truths in my studies of physics. I will endeavor to explain some of what I have discovered about God's eternal power and divine nature as we go through this book.

I was often entertained in my college classes, as the professor would say something that corresponded directly with a Bible verse. I find it interesting that God is all over the place in science, but many scientists rarely notice the correlation. It made perfect sense to me that they would correspond. Both the Bible and Creation were written by the same Author. So, everything they say must be consistent.

Of course, we don't fully understand what creation has to say yet. Science only understands the most basic principles of how God made everything, and most of the scientists don't actually want to admit that. We still have a long way to go. The more we explore nature, the more we learn. It would be shear arrogance to say that we actually fully understand anything about the laws of nature. We have a good foundational understanding of the core principles. However, there are so many details that still remain a mystery.

Many of us like to think that we really understand the Bible and what God is saying through it. But, I doubt that anyone actually fully understands it. All of our endless debates about what the Scriptures are really saying just demonstrate how little we really understand it. We may have a basic understanding of the core principles, but God is constantly revealing more of the depths of His character and nature to us through the Scriptures.

The more we study both the Bible and the Creation, the more we learn about God and about His character, power, and nature. We have already learned so much, but there is so much more we can learn. We need to maintain some humility about what we know and what we don't know and always be teachable. There are many mysteries that we are on the verge of discovering and understanding. However, many more mysteries are way too far beyond our ability to ever understand.

Because there is so much that we don't understand about science and about the Bible, we have a tendency to think that they conflict with each other. However, it's impossible for them to actually conflict since they were both written by God. God is way too brilliant and detail oriented to miss something and leave a loophole or an inconsistency in His creation or His words. There is no way that our little brains could think of anything that God in all His brilliance hasn't already thought of. Therefore, any conflict or paradox between the laws of nature and the Scriptures is on our side because of our limited understanding.

When we come across a paradox, we tend to get stuck there. We have two things that are both true but seem to be conflicting with each other. We don't know what to do with that, so we either pick one side over the other or just say we don't get it. However, a paradox is not a wall meant to stop us; it is a doorway inviting us to higher understanding. A paradox is an invitation to gain a deeper understanding of how the two sides are simultaneously true. Once we gain that understanding, we can move beyond the conflict and the taking of sides and can fully embrace the multifaceted truth that is being revealed in the paradox.

One paradox we are faced with concerns miracles and physics. When we don't understand enough about God and His ways or about the laws of physics to resolve the paradox, we are often tempted to take sides. We either decide to believe that miracles don't actually happen and they are just myths or tricks, or we decide to believe that God is breaking or superseding the laws of physics when He does a miracle. Many people don't understand how both miracles and physics can peacefully and simultaneously coexist.

As we will see throughout this book, the laws of physics and nature are extremely flexible and versatile. They allow for many possibilities well beyond what we normally think of as physically possible. One of the reasons why quantum physics is so weird (and cool in my opinion) is that there are so many phenomena that don't make any common sense and seem physically impossible, but those same phenomena make miracles very easy. We will talk more about that throughout the book. My point, for now, is that the laws of physics don't need to be broken or superseded for God to perform any of the miracles recorded in the Bible and those happening currently.

Also, just because there is a natural explanation for a miracle doesn't mean that God isn't responsible for causing it. For example, think about the game of Roulette. It is physically possible to win Roulette ten times in a row. No laws of nature need to be broken for that extremely rare event to happen. It's not impossible, but no one is going to believe that someone is just that "lucky." That sequence of events is so unlikely, that there has to be something manipulating the rules to make it happen. God does that when He does miracles. He makes highly improbable but not impossible events actually happen. If it actually happened, it is possible within the laws of nature. Even if we have no idea how it is possible, if it happened, it is possible.

Holding fast to the laws of physics doesn't imply that miracles don't happen. Likewise, holding fast to the truth and accuracy of the Biblical miracles doesn't mean that the laws of physics as we understand them aren't also true. In fact, God says that He won't break the laws of nature in the Bible.[1] He created nature and the laws that govern it. God is very smart and planned out the whole universe before He started. He made the rules to allow for everything that He ever wanted to do. Plus, it is not in God's nature to break His own laws.[2]

> *Jeremiah 33:25-26 ESV, "Thus says the LORD: If I have not established my covenant with day and night and the fixed order of heaven and earth, then I will reject the offspring of Jacob and David my servant and will not choose one of his offspring to rule over the offspring of Abraham, Isaac, and Jacob. For I will restore their fortunes and will have mercy on them."*

In this verse, we see that God made a covenant with the fixed order and laws of heaven and earth (the laws of both the unseen and seen realms). The laws that govern how heaven and earth work aren't just some rules that God plays fast and loose with. The laws of nature are fixed and established as firmly as the covenant that God made with Abraham, Isaac, and Jacob. We all know that God does not break His covenants. We break them all the time, but God never does. God will never break His covenant with Abraham, Isaac, and Jacob. God will also never break His covenant with the fixed laws of His Creation.

---

[1] Psalms 148:1-6, Jeremiah 31:35-36, 33:20-22
[2] Genesis 17:4-9, Leviticus 26:44-45, Numbers 23:19, Psalms 89:28-35, 111:7-9, Isaiah 55:3, Jeremiah 32:38-41

I find this verse very reassuring. It tells me that God is knowable and consistent. He isn't like all those other gods in ancient times. In the stories and myths, those other gods were always changing and doing so many unpredictable things. They were never constant, unchanging, or knowable like the God of the Bible. God is so much smarter than we could ever comprehend and His ways are higher than our ways[3] so there are facets of God that we will never be able to understand or predict. But, the God of the Bible wants us to know Him and makes Himself able to be known by us. One of the ways He does that is by being consistent and unchanging.[4] We can't learn about or understand something that is always changing. However, God is always the same, so we can learn about Him and His ways.

God put that facet of His character into the laws He made to govern the Universe too. So, we can know the laws of physics, because they are constant and unchanging. God doesn't go around messing with them all the time. Studying science is actually possible according to the Bible, and it even seems encouraged in these verses. I appreciate that as a scientist.

The more I studied about physics, the more I saw how well God's Word and God's creation were perfectly integrated. There is no actual conflict between science and the Bible. However, there is often conflict between people and our interpretations of science and the Bible. I have found that most of that conflict has to do with misunderstandings

---

[3] Isaiah 55:9
[4] Hebrews 13:8, Numbers 23:19, 1 Samuel 15:29

and misinterpretations of what the other side is saying. Both sides are speaking different languages and the translation between them is often filled with false assumptions and prejudices.

If we have to pick one side of the paradox or the other, there is always going to be a conflict between the science minded and the Christian minded. However, since science and the Bible both work together and don't conflict at all in reality, there is hope that we can all get along and even work together to discover more about God's amazing character and nature.

My heart has always been to help the two sides better communicate with each other. The Bible and science are actually saying the same things. We just don't really understand what either is saying perfectly yet. There is no need for the two groups to be fighting and rejecting each other. I would like to contribute to the reconciliation between the Christian minded and the science minded.

Dad always said that really smart people can always communicate with everyone at their level. People who are really smart can explain anything using small and simple words because they actually understand what they are talking about and whom they are talking to. It is shear arrogance and insecurity to use big words to try to impress people and convince them that one is smart. Talking over people's heads is often a self-centered way to boost the speaker's ego. Although sometimes, people will use big words because that is how they were trained and they don't know any other way to explain what they are trying to explain. But, good teaching is all about helping the listener and doing whatever we can to help them understand in their own way at their own level.

So, we grew up learning not to talk over people's heads. We want to talk directly with them in a way they can understand. Otherwise, we are just wasting our words and not actually helping anyone. As I felt God calling me to pursue a ministry of teaching others about God and science, I have also been learning more and more ways to communicate with people at their level so they can fully understand everything I am teaching. If the reader doesn't understand what I am saying then I have failed at my job. It is my greatest desire for each and every reader to learn more about God and His love for them through what God has given me to teach so that each and every person can grow and be blessed to connect to God in a deeper and more intimate way.

In this book, I will explain some of the things I have found in physics that correspond well with what the Bible really says. My hope is that the reader will be encouraged and blessed and gain a deeper understanding of who God is and what He is like as revealed through His Word and through His Creation.

I don't want anyone to be intimidated by the subject of science and God. I have tried to simplify these concepts down as much as I can. I believe that there is something here for everyone to learn and understand whether you are a science minded person or a Christian minded person or both. I have included many footnotes with extra science information for those who want to dig deeper in to the science side. I have also included many footnotes with further Scripture references for those who want to dig deeper into the Bible side. Or, you can skip all the footnotes and just try to grasp the essence of what I have discovered about God and the way that He made the universe.

Regardless of your level of interest in science and regardless of what you believe about your ability to learn, I hope you will learn something more about who God is, how He made you, and how He made the universe. I pray that you allow God to speak to you through what He has shown me through His Creation as you read through this book.

at the time. Then, we get more data and understanding, which sometimes makes an old theory obsolete. However, we usually don't throw out the old theories entirely. We refine them and build upon them.

We wouldn't have any modern science without building on the shoulders of all those who have gone before. Without the ancient Greek philosophers and mathematicians, we wouldn't have any modern technology. They were very limited and naïve in their theories. They believed a lot of crazy stuff. But, they weren't totally wrong either. We simply kept the good parts and let go of the rest.

As you read through this book, you may encounter some new information that will challenge some of your current theories about how the world works. I encourage you to hold your theories lightly and let them be refined as God helps you sort through what I am sharing and how that relates to what you believe about how the physical and spiritual world works. Keep the good and let go of the rest.

Visible vs. Invisible

Over many millennia of studying nature by observations and experiments, we have learned all kinds of things about chemistry, biology, and physics. However, for most of history, all of our observations and experiments have been limited to what we could see with the naked eye or possibly by looking through a telescope or a microscope. Until the last hundred and fifty years or so, human eyes along with our other senses were the only detectors we had to work with.

So, all of our conclusions and intuition were entirely based on what we perceived through our five senses.

That level of understanding is called Classical Mechanics. It includes principles like Newton's laws. Things fall. Things bounce. Big, heavy things are harder to move than small, light things. Things always come into balance. These things all form our human intuition. Even small babies know that things fall and will try to catch themselves.

When Newton developed the math (calculus) to describe these commonly understood phenomena, we finally had the ability to dive deeper into understanding the actual mechanics of how everything works beyond our intuition. Once we had math, we could make predictions about the future and plan for it. We no longer had to be powerless victims of the forces of nature just dealing with whatever happened after the fact. With math and physics, we can plan and prepare for the future.

Having calculus was a huge leap forward for science, but we were still limited by observing with only our five senses. Then, some very smart people developed sensors that could detect things we couldn't see.[1] We could finally detect infinitesimally small things like electrons, photons, and other quantum particles that couldn't be seen with any traditional

---

[1] There are many different types of detectors that help us "see" the unseen such as photo-detectors, Geiger counters and other radiation detectors, tunneling electron microscopes, compasses, radio antennas, voltmeters, bubble chambers, cloud chambers, scintillators, and other particle detectors. And, there are also many other types of detectors scientists use to measure quantum particles, quantum effects, and quantum fields.

microscope. Quantum Mechanics was developed to study those tiny things that couldn't be seen normally and to find math to describe and predict them. Good math is absolutely vital when studying things that you can't see.

This caused a revolution in our ability to study the physics of the invisible part of the universe. Then, everything changed in our understanding of the laws that governed nature. None of the data from the invisible part of the universe made any sense. All the behavior we were discovering about what we couldn't see (like electrons) completely contradicted our intuition and understanding of the natural behavior of all that we could see in the world around us.

At first, it seemed impossible to reconcile the behavior we were detecting in the unseen/invisible realm with the behavior we observe in the visible realm. Everything seemed like one paradox after another. Every scientist had their own theory about what might be going on. Many of those early, naïve theories became quite popular in various circles like sci-fi. After a long time and a lot of work by a lot of very smart people, we pared down all the wild initial hypotheses and developed theories that were more sophisticated. We have finally just begun to be able to understand how both the visible and invisible realms work together.

We can now finally explain some of the crazy phenomena of the unseen/invisible realm that quantum physics has discovered. Before we can discuss those things, we need to lay a proper foundation and talk about the basic principles of what everything is made out of – the substance

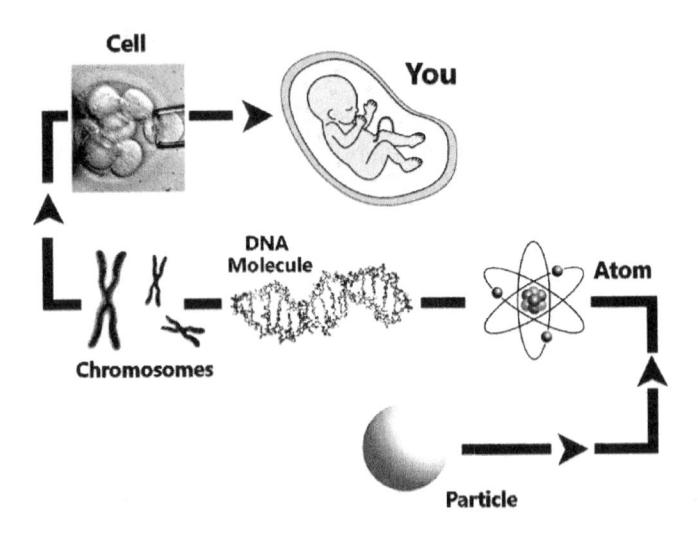

Figure 1: The building blocks of all people and everything else are quantum particles.

of reality. Then, we can build on that foundation to talk about the more complex, strange, and counter-intuitive phenomena we find in the unseen realm.

Quantum Particles

So, what is everything in the universe made out of? Well, there are visible light and other forms of electromagnetic radiation like x-rays, radio waves, and microwaves. Those are all the same thing, just at different frequencies, and they are all made out of photons. Photons don't take up any space and don't have any mass, so they are not in the category of "matter". However, they do have lots of energy and momentum.

On the other hand, we also have all the matter in the universe. That is all the solid stuff that takes up space and has mass; things like people, animals, plants, rocks, planets, and stars. All living things are made out of cells. Inside each cell, there are a bunch of protein molecules, DNA molecules, and other kinds of molecules. Each molecule is made up of lots of different kinds of atoms like carbon, hydrogen, and oxygen. The non-living matter is also made up of molecules and atoms like gold, iron, and silicon. So, all the bulky matter in the universe is made out of atoms of various kinds (see Figure 1). To give you a sense of scale, the average atom is one ten-millionth of a millimeter in diameter. That means that ten million atoms lined up end-to-end can fit inside one millimeter. They are pretty tiny.

Now, inside the atoms there are electrons flying around the outside orbiting the nucleus sort of like the earth orbits the sun. However, the electrons don't stay in a nice elliptical plane the way the planets do. They are going all around in a sphere and several other complex three-dimensional shapes. The tiny electrons are whizzing around so fast in such a complicated orbit, that it looks a lot like a fuzzy cloud. In fact, we can't quite tell where the electron exactly is. We can't even tell how big the electron is. It is so tiny and always moving so fast that we can't measure its size. The atoms are very tiny (one ten-millionth of a millimeter), and the electrons are much, much smaller.

Inside the nucleus of the atom are protons and neutrons. Inside each of those, are three quarks apiece. The quarks are so small that we can't really measure how big they are either. There are over a hundred different chemical elements that make up all the matter in the universe. The only real difference among them is how many protons and matching electrons they have. Some have more and some have less. The only difference between gold and iron is a few protons.

Each atom is made up of electrons, quarks, and a few other exotic particles like gluons. There are just a small set of these particles, called quantum particles, which make up all the matter in the universe. Photons and a few other massless particles are also in the set of quantum particles.[2] Therefore, everything in the universe whether it is solid or not is made out of quantum particles.

Quantum Waves

Then, are the quantum particles the substance of reality, or are they made out of something else? It turns out that they are made out of something else. The electrons, photons, and whatnot are made out of quantum waves. Quantum waves are things like electromagnetic waves, gravity waves, and some others we haven't even named yet. The simplest and easiest to understand example of a quantum wave is an electromagnetic wave. We all have some familiarity with electricity and magnetism. Electricity is what is flowing through the circuitry in our homes to power the lights, computers, and all our electronics. And, we've all probably played with magnets or a compass at one time or another.

---

[2] The full set of quantum particles that make up everything is called the Standard Model. You can think of it like the periodic table for quantum particles.

Let's look at how magnets work for a moment to help us understand more about the electromagnetic field. When you have two magnets with the same poles facing each other, they repel each other, and you have to work hard to push them together. If the poles are different, they attract each other, and you have to work hard to pull them apart. The same is true for electrically charged objects like electrons. Like charges repel. Opposite charges attract. But, the magnets and charges never touch each other. They pull and push on each other without ever touching. So, they must be interacting through something that does not require physical contact. That something is called the electromagnetic force field. When a magnet or charge moves, it creates a disturbance in the force field that causes the field to shake like ripples in a pond.

Think of it like moving a stick through some water. The stick will make waves in the water. If we move the stick quickly, the waves will shake quickly and the ripples will be close together (high frequency). If we move the stick slowly, the waves in the water will shake slowly and the ripples will be more spread out (low frequency). The same thing happens with all waves. If a magnetic or charged object moves quickly back and forth, it will make high frequency waves in the electromagnetic field. If it moves slowly, it will make low frequency waves.

When the waves come across another magnetic or charged particle, that one will start shaking too. It is just like when water waves hit a buoy and it bobs up and down with the wave. All waves impart energy to whatever they hit and make that thing move in the same way as the wave. A high frequency wave will shake what it hits very quickly and a low frequency wave will shake it slowly.

That is why high frequency electromagnetic waves, like x-rays and certain kinds of radiation, are so dangerous. They have a lot of energy and shake small things like our cells way too fast, which kills the cells. However, low frequency electromagnetic waves like radio waves don't have as much energy and only shake big things relatively slowly. Therefore, they don't cause damage. Waves can only shake objects that are about the same size as its wavelength (how far it moves before completing one cycle back and forth) or about the size of a multiple of its wavelength.

Contrary to some popular opinions, high frequencies are bad and low frequencies are good. Think about it like this, would you rather have someone rock you slowly and gently, or shake you quickly and violently? Which one is more peaceful and restful? Which state is better to pursue? In fact, everything in nature wants to go to the lowest frequency and thus the lowest energy state that it can reach. If there is a way to drop to a lower energy/frequency state, every quantum particle will do so. Everything in nature wants to be in the ground state where it is at rest as much as it can be.[3]

It takes a so much work to drive a quantum particle or anything bigger into a higher energy state and keep it there.

---

[3] The ground state for a macroscopic object is completely at rest; it is not moving. For a quantum particle, the ground state is still waving, but at the lowest allowed frequency. In other words, it is vibrating as slowly as possible.

You wouldn't want to hold this book above your head for very long, would you? You would want to drop it as soon as you could. It takes a lot of energy to keep it up there in that higher energy state. Everything in nature agrees: lower energy and thus lower frequencies are better and easier. The rest state is better than the excited state. Everything in nature flows to the lowest point (the least energy).

So, don't listen to anyone telling you how you are supposed to be accessing the higher frequency bands of whatever. That is completely unnatural and totally contrary to the way all of nature works. If you try to get to higher frequencies, everything in nature both physical and nonphysical will fight you. There is only rest and peace in the lowest energy state not in any higher energy state. Low frequencies mean calm, rest, and stability just like a father gently rocking a sleeping baby. High frequencies mean agitation, tension, and instability like a toddler bouncing off the walls. Which one would you rather be?

Quantum waves are waves. So, they have the properties that are common to all waves. They have constant amplitude (how high the wave is) and frequency (how fast it is oscillating). Quantum waves are transverse waves called "plane waves" because they travel in one direction, but they vibrate in other directions (see Figure 2). Thus, the wave front propagates out from the source in a plane.

Electromagnetic waves are also spread out like all waves. You can think about it just like a water wave. The water vibrates up and down, but the wave moves across the surface. How big is a water wave? And, where is it? It is all

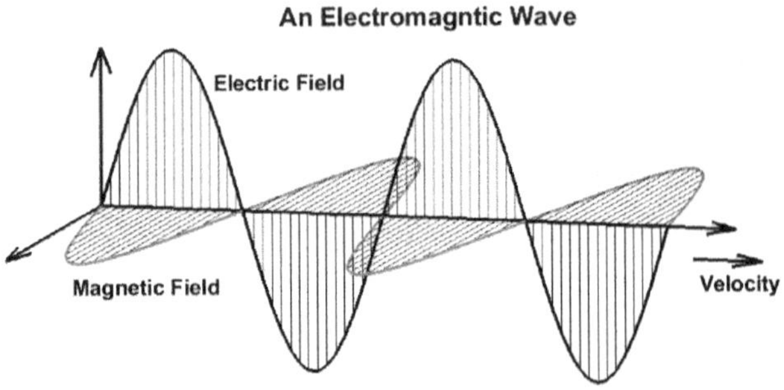

An Electromagntic Wave

Figure 2: In an electromagnetic wave like light, the electric and magnetic fields vibrate in perpendicular directions to the direction of movement.

over, not just in one place. Plus, it's always moving. Therefore, we can't lock it down in any one place or say how big it is. All the quantum waves, like light and all the others, are like that too.

Interference

Now, I just said that the infinitesimally tiny quantum particles, like electrons, are made out of quantum waves, which are all spread out all over the place. That seems contradictory, doesn't it? This is the first paradox we encounter when learning about quantum physics. It is called "Wave-Particle Duality." That means that all the quantum particles sometimes behave like a billiard ball – localized and bouncing off each other like a ball would. Sometimes, the quantum particles behave like waves – spread out and interfering with each other. And, sometimes they do both at the same time! So, how does that work? Like all paradoxes, there is a way to resolve this one too. I will give a brief

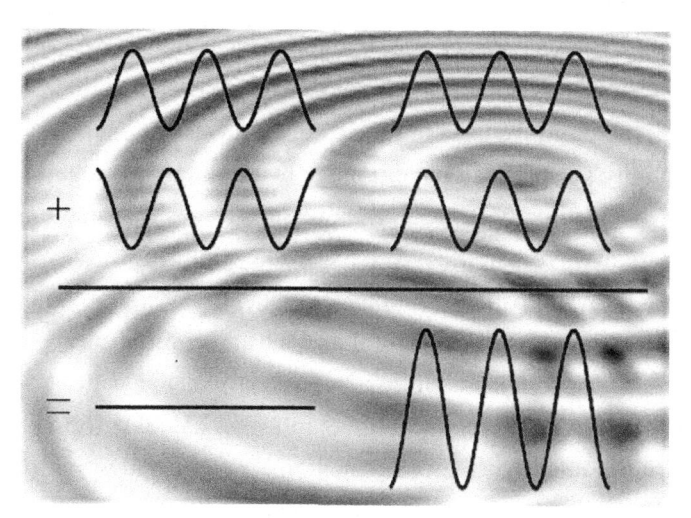

Figure 3: Ripples in water show interference in the waves. The interference is just simple addition.

overview here, but we will discuss this phenomenon in more detail in chapter 6. First, we need to know a little more about how waves work.

Waves interact with each other by interference. We've all seen interference at work in the ripples in a pond (see Figure 3). The waves spread out from a rock or whatever splashed into the water. The ripples spread out evenly in all directions. When the ripples come across another set of ripples, they interfere with each other. When two peaks overlap, they add up and make a higher peak. When, two valleys overlap they combine and make a deeper valley. When a peak and a valley overlap, they cancel each other out and the result is flat. Interference is just simple addition. Two positives add up to make a bigger positive; two negatives subtract to make a bigger negative; and a positive and a negative cancel each other out. This behavior we see in water waves is universal. It applies to all waves.

One thing we need to notice about interference is that we can only see the total pattern made by all the waves together. We can't directly detect the individual waves that make up the total wave pattern. We have to use math to deconstruct the total wave pattern into the component waves. For simple patterns, like the one in Figure 3, the component wave patterns are obvious. But, for very complicated patterns, it takes some very creative and complicated calculus formulas to figure out what the component waves are.[4] However, we don't need to worry about how complicated it can get. We'll leave that to the experts and their computer programs to deal with. We're going to keep things simple here. Just remember we can only directly observe the total pattern and never the individual component patterns.

Now, when we add waves of frequencies that are close together, it forms a beat. Take, for example, the case where someone is tuning a guitar. They play the reference frequency for the note. Then, they pluck the string and hear a beat. The two frequencies are close together, so when they interfere with each other, sometimes the waves add up and sometimes they cancel. We only hear the total wave pattern, which is going up and down as the adding and canceling happens. That's why we hear a beat. When the string gets

---

[4] The most common method for deconstructing a wave pattern into its component waves is called a Fourier transform. It involves an integral transform (calculus). The Fourier transform is frequently used in electronics, software, mathematics, and physics.

Individual Waves

Interference (3 Waves)

Wave Packet (Many Waves)

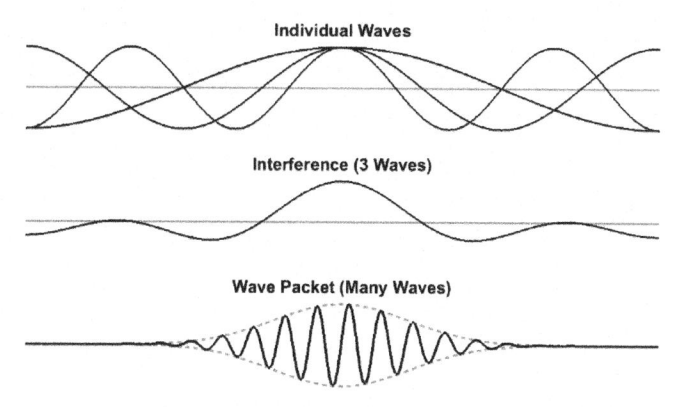

Figure 4: Wave interference adds up to make a wave packet. This is just a 2D schematic drawing. Real quantum particles are waving in all the dimensions.

perfectly in sync with the reference frequency, the two waves are the same, so they always add up and never cancel. Then, the beat pattern goes away and the guitar is tuned.

If we add up many waves, we can get some very interesting wave patterns. We can get square waves, pulses, and saw-tooth waveforms just to name a few. We can even get a wave pattern that is high in one place and cancels out everywhere else like a bell curve (see Figure 4). The waving is mostly localized in the middle of the bell curve. However, in the tails, there isn't hardly any waving happening.

Wave Packets

Recall that we were talking about how localized quantum particles are formed out of spread out quantum waves. That basically works by interfering the quantum waves in a very specific way to get a localized "wave packet" that looks and acts a lot like a tiny billiard ball.

In quantum physics, all particles are really wave packets. They are tiny and mostly localized, but they are also waving very quickly in many different directions. This makes them look like fuzzy little balls when we measure them. We often picture them as little clouds. Clouds are a good analogy here. They aren't exactly solid, and we don't know exactly where the cloud has an edge. We can see it and measure some things about it, but we can't quite get a handle on it. How big is it? Where is it? And, how fast is it going? These are very difficult questions to answer when it comes to quantum particles even though these are perfectly normal questions in the macroscopic (things we can see) world.

It took scientists quite a long time to become comfortable with the fact that those basic questions can't really be answered in the unseen quantum world. Some scientists still struggle with it. So, don't worry about it, if you have some trouble getting comfortable these concepts.

It makes sense, though, that those would be difficult questions when we think about how the particles are made out of waves. Waves are spread out as far as they can be, so it doesn't make any sense to ask where a wave is or how big it is. When you ask nonsensical questions, you get nonsensical answers. On the other hand, the wave packet is fairly localized, so you can get an idea of where it is and how big it is. But, it is still not a point or a solid ball that has a specific location and size.

We can tell how fast a single wave is oscillating very easily. However, there are many waves making up the wave packet of the quantum particle and each one has a different frequency. Frequency is the main factor in quantum momentum,[5] which is what we actually measure for quantum particles. There is a wide range of momenta in each wave packet, so it doesn't make any sense to ask for one momentum (frequency) for the total wave packet.

That's the problem with most of our experiments: we are asking for one answer when there is really a range of answers. In the macroscopic world, there is frequently only one correct answer. In the quantum world, there is never just one correct answer; the correct answer is always a distribution (a weighted set of answers).

The problem is that we can only measure the answers to our experimental questions with macroscopic equipment, which can only report one answer at a time. This can lead to a lot of confusion when we try to interpret the results. We are usually interpreting the data as though the quantum wave packets are either a particle or a wave. However, in reality, they are both particle-like and wave-like at the same time. They are wave packets, which have some particle properties and some wave properties. We always want to look for both/and questions and answers not either/or questions.

We have all these of quantum waves that are combining together to make up fuzzy little clouds that we call quantum

---

[5] In classical physics, momentum = mass * velocity. This formula only works for particles with mass. In quantum physics, momentum = h/c * frequency, where h is Plank's constant and c is the speed of light. This formula works for waves that don't have mass. Frequency is how many wave peaks pass a point in one second. This is a type of "speed" for waves. Therefore, we have a constant multiplied by a type of speed for both equations.

particles. Those quantum particles, like electrons, quarks, and photons, make up all the matter and light in the universe. Therefore, ultimately everything is made out of all these quantum waves.

Waving in What?

The next natural question is to ask what these quantum waves are waving in? Water waves wave in water. Sound waves wave in air. What do the quantum waves wave in? Whatever that substance is makes up everything in the universe whether light or matter. That is the substance of reality.

When scientists first started pondering this question back in the late 1800s, they named the substance that light waves were waving in "the Ether."[6] Light waves are the easiest quantum waves to perform experiments on, as they are simply electromagnetic waves. Remember, however, that there are other kinds of quantum waves too. Once they had a name, like good scientists, they tried to find out as much as they could about the characteristics and substance of the Ether.

In 1885, Michelson and Morley conducted their famous experiment[7] to determine how light was affected by the

---

[6] It is also sometimes spelled Aether or Æther and sometimes called the Luminiferous Ether.

[7] Michelson, Albert A.; Morley, Edward W. (1887). "On the Relative Motion of the Earth and the Luminiferous Ether". American Journal of Science 34: 333–345. doi:10.2475/ajs.s3-34.203.333

movement of the earth through space. They were trying to discover how much of a wake the earth was making in the Ether the way a boat would make a wake in water. They figured that the light that was moving in the same direction that the earth was moving in would wave differently than the light that was moving across the wake sideways (i.e., the light traveling sideways would travel more slowly and/or be distorted).

However, that is not what they found at all. They found that there was no wake in the Ether at all, and that the light didn't care what direction it was moving in. The speed of light in a vacuum was constant. Now, we've all been taught that all of our lives, so that's not a shocking thought to us. But, for them it rocked their world-view and made them reevaluate their entire understanding about how the universe works. Most people don't understand the consequences of having a constant speed of light. They think it is just a random fact that has no relevance to their lives. However, understanding the consequences might just rock your world-view too.

The thing is that since there is no wake in the Ether to change the speed of light, it shows that the Ether isn't physically affected by the earth or anything else. We now know that the Ether is just the electromagnetic field, which doesn't interact by touching as we already discussed. It doesn't physically interact with anything because there isn't anything physically there. The electromagnetic field (Ether) doesn't physically exist! We have since proved this in many other ways by many other experiments. The electromagnetic field interacts electromagnetically with electromagnetic objects, but there is no physical interaction and no physical substance. There are just a whole lot of waves that are moving everything in the universe around and building up the quantum particles.

Think about the consequences of this. It's like having a water wave with no water! We can measure the light wave and all of its properties. Everyone can see the light and measures it the same way. However, there isn't any measurable substance there to be waving. But, how can light be waving in nothing? We can all see the light. It is right here bouncing off the page and into your eyes. Light is real. We all know that light exists, but light is not physical at all. Light is a wave in the nonphysical electromagnetic field. Therefore, it is a nonphysical wave. This was very disturbing to the scientific community at the time, and it still is today to some extent.

True Substance

Think about it for a moment. You are made out of cells, which are made out of atoms. Everything else is made out of atoms too. Those atoms are made out of electrons, quarks, and some other quantum particles. Those quantum particles are made out of quantum waves interfering to make tiny wave packets (see Figure 5). So, that means that you and the rest of the universe are made out of quantum particles, which are made out of quantum waves, which are waving in nothing!

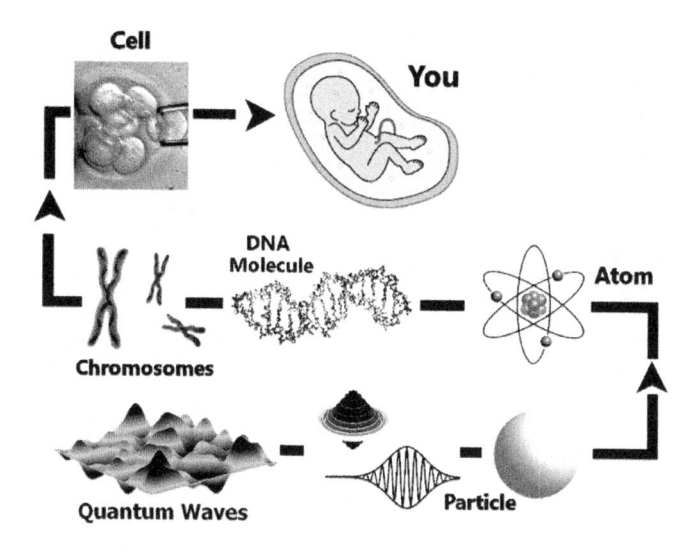

Figure 5: Everything is made out of quantum waves, which are waving in nothing (physical).

Therefore, the universe is made out of nothing! And somehow, the nothing is waving and making something! Now, what or who is waving the nothing and making the something, hmm? Likewise, you are made out of nothing, or at least, nothing that is physically observable. That is, you are made out of nothing physical; you are made out of something nonphysical. You and everything else are made out of waving nonphysical quantum fields. Therefore, the nonphysical quantum fields are the substance of reality.

We normally think that the solid objects we see and touch are substantive, but when we look closely at the solid objects, they stop being solid. They are simply fuzzy clouds of waving nonphysical quantum fields squished into three-dimensional shapes that repel other nonphysical fuzzy clouds through nonphysical forces.

Think about touch in this context. The atoms in the skin of my finger have negatively charged electrons whirling around the outside of them making a three-dimensional cloud of waving nonphysical quantum fields. The atoms of the page of this book also have negatively charged electrons whirling around on the outside of them making up their three-dimensional shapes. The two negative charges repel each other and push against each other through the electromagnetic force. At some very short distance, I don't have enough energy to push the two sets of negative charges in my finger and the page any closer together. So, my finger stops, and my brain interprets that as "touching" the "solid" page. When in reality, it's just a complicated force field repelling another complicated force field.

Since this is the case, what is actually substantive? Does the wave pattern that you can see have the substance in it or does the stuff that is waving have more substance? In order to better understand what the substance of reality actually is, I think it will be helpful to define "substance" here. The dictionary defines substance[8] as "essential nature or essence; a fundamental or characteristic part or quality; ultimate reality that underlies all outward manifestations and change; practical importance, meaning, usefulness; physical material from which something is made or which has discrete

---

[8] "substance." Merriam-Webster.com. Merriam-Webster, 2015. Web. 9 April 2015.

existence; matter of particular or definite chemical constitution."

We are used to thinking of the atoms that make up solid objects as the substance of the objects, which agrees with the last part of the definition. We tend to think that if we can see and touch something that it has substance. But, we also talk about the substance of immaterial things, like the substance of an idea, argument, or opinion, or like the substance of a person's character. These examples get to the first part of the definition: the essence of something. Therefore, we have physical and nonphysical meanings for the word substance.

Scientifically, the middle definition, "ultimate reality that underlies all outward manifestations and change" is the one that is the most relevant. Quantum fields are what underlie all the rapidly changing waves that make up the manifested wave packets (particles). The fields themselves don't ever change. They are constant and pervasive. They are everywhere and always the same everywhere. The electrons, quarks, and photons are the outward manifestations. The quantum fields are the unseen reality that underlies everything physical and observable.

Think again about the waves in the ocean. They are always moving and changing. The boats, surfers, beach-goers, and weather forecasters care a lot about the ocean waves and the patterns they make. All of our lives and actions are affected greatly by the patterns of the ocean waves. Do the waves themselves have substance, or is it the ocean water that has substance? Which one is more constant, stable, and dependable? Which one is the changing outward manifestation and which one the underling reality? The ocean waves derive their substance from the ocean. It is the same with quantum particles. The substance of the physical electrons, quarks, photons, etc. is derived from the underlying nonphysical substance of the quantum fields.

So far, quantum physics has discovered that the substance of all reality is an unseen, nonphysical substance that we call quantum force fields (like the electromagnetic field, gravity field, etc.). Quantum physics has also discovered that everything observable and physical is a manifestation of that unseen, nonphysical substance. The Bible says the same thing, as we would expect, since it was written by the same Author who created nature:

> *Hebrews 11:1, 3, "Now faith is confidence in what we hope for and assurance about what we do not see. ... By faith we understand that the universe was formed at God's command, so that what is seen was not made out of what was visible."*

This verse seems fairly straightforward. It says that what can be seen (observable, physical things) was made out of the unseen (non-observable, non-physical) just as scientists have been discovering.

In the Beginning

Let's look back at what God said about the beginning of creation and see what He has to say in relation to all of this:

Genesis 1:1-2 NASB, "In the beginning God created the heavens and the earth. The earth was formless and void, and darkness was over the surface of the deep, and the Spirit of God was moving over the surface of the waters."

The Hebrew word translated "moving" can also be translated shaking or fluttering. The imagery is that of a mother bird lovingly brooding and fluttering over her young. We see here that, in the beginning, the Spirit of God is shaking and vibrating the formless void and creating the heavens and the earth.

The "formless void" is what we call "the vacuum" in science. It exists in outer space where there is nothing physical and it exists in the empty space between the atoms and other particles. The vacuum is everywhere, but the vacuum is far from empty. It is empty of anything physical, but it is full of the nonphysical quantum waves shaking and vibrating wildly in every possible way.[9]

The Hebrew word for "face" in the verse above is the literal face of a person or object, or the person or object's image and countenance. When we picture the vacuum in our

---

[9] Occasionally, quantum particle-antiparticle pairs will pop out of the vacuum as the interference of the waves temporarily causes a pair of wave packets to form. Then, the particle and anti-particles annihilate each other and go back into the vacuum. This happens on a very short timescale and the masses are so small that we can't really measure them. Therefore, we tend to believe that outer space is empty, but it is only empty of stable physical particles. Outer space is full of nonphysical quantum fields that are violently waving in unstable, constantly changing patterns.

minds or show it in an illustration, it has the image and countenance of water waves. It is the closest analogy and picture we have. That is why I have been using that analogy repeatedly.

In the beginning of the universe, the latest research says that there was only the formless void of the vacuum vibrating wildly all over. Then, as the universe expanded and cooled down, stable wave packets of particles started forming which created the physical electrons, quarks, and whatnot. Then, those combined together to make the atoms and all the matter that we have now.

Science and the Bible agree about these first moments of creation. At first, there was a formless void that was being waved like water. Then, the waves were vibrated and combined in a very specific, precisely engineered way to make the Heavens and the Earth, that is, everything in Creation.

The Scripture says that God not only created and directed the waving of quantum fields to make everything, but He did so like a loving and caring mother bird. He was carefully and fully attentive to the needs of His children, brooding over every minute detail to get it just right. I'm awestruck at how much God loves us and connects with us in the very depths of our being and by how much God connects with all of Creation.

Sustaining

Let's take a look at some of the other scriptures on this topic and see what they have to say about how God interacts with the quantum waves in the universe and about God's character and nature.

> *Hebrews 1:2-3a, "but in these last days he has spoken to us by his Son, whom he appointed heir of all things, and through whom also he made the universe. The Son is the radiance of God's glory and the exact representation of his being, sustaining all things by his powerful word."*
>
> *Colossians 1:15-17, "The Son is the image of the invisible God, the firstborn over all creation. For in him all things were created: things in heaven and on earth, visible and invisible, whether thrones or powers or rulers or authorities; all things have been created through him and for him. He is before all things, and in him all things hold together."*

We see here God reaffirming His creation of the universe through His Son, Jesus. We also see that Jesus is sustaining all things by His powerful word and holding all things together. Now, God is Spirit and His words are spirit.[10] Therefore, we aren't talking about physical words like those that we say to each other. When we speak, it produces vibrations in the air that propagate through the medium of the air and then strike someone else's eardrum, which then causes the listener's eardrum to vibrate in the same way as

---

[10] John 4:24, 6:63, Romans 8:26, 1 Corinthians 2:12-13

the speaker's voice. In normal talking, the speaker's voice and the listener's ear come into sync with each other. But, English isn't God's native language! God speaks in spiritual words that move spiritual things. Spiritual vibrations in a spiritual medium will move out and cause a change in whatever the waves hit to bring the recipient into sync with the source.

The Bible is frequently talking about spiritual things all over the place. It talks about the spiritual realm itself (Heaven and Hell[11]), spiritual beings (angels and demons), human spirits, and God's Holy Spirit. The Bible also clearly differentiates the physical realm (visible) from the spiritual realm (invisible). There is no mention of any other realms in the Bible. And, what else could there be anyway?

Science hasn't discovered anything about nonphysical beings yet, but we are starting to discover many things about the nonphysical (invisible) realm itself. We've been discussing that throughout this chapter. The nonphysical realm is the realm of quantum waves (light, gravity, etc.) in quantum force fields and of higher dimensions (which we will discuss in more detail in the next chapter). Science is just taking its first steps towards discovering all the

---

[11] The first Heaven traditionally refers to outer space, the stars, and the rest of the universe beyond the skies of earth. The second heaven traditionally refers to the Hell zone of creation, that is, the dominion/kingdom of Satan. The third heaven traditionally refers to the Heaven zone of creation, that is, the dominion/kingdom of God. The first heaven is a physical zone. The second and third heavens are nonphysical zones. The tradition is based on the verses in 2 Corinthians 12:2-4.

principles of the nonphysical realm. There is still so much more to discover. The latest research says we have the physical realm and the nonphysical realm. There are only those two. Therefore, we can easily identify the nonphysical realm that science talks about with the spiritual realm that the Bible talks about.

So, what would happen scientifically, when God speaks in spiritual/nonphysical words? It causes vibrations in the quantum fields that travel along and interfere with the other vibrations making complex patterns and causing changes. When the vibrations hit an object, they will bring that object into sync with the source, with God's words, just like our ear drums come into sync with the speaker's voice.

Remember that physical and nonphysical vibrations are just waves on a membrane. There is nothing weird or mystical about it. When you shake something, it shakes. Then, it shakes its neighbors, and the next things shake too. And, so on as the wave propagates outward shaking things as it goes. It's a fairly simple principle. So, don't let people try to confuse you about it and try to sell you all kinds of weird ideas about spiritual vibrations. All waves behave the same way. If someone is trying to convince you about something that doesn't make sense for a water wave, it doesn't make sense for a spiritual wave either.

The complex patterns in the quantum fields that are formed by God's words could create the wave packets that make up the quantum particles that make up all things. And/or, they could cause the particles to move around or change states. We don't know exactly, but Hebrews 1:3

states that Jesus is constantly sustaining all things. That implies that He is sustaining the waving of the quantum waves, which make up all things and their movements and energy states.

Let's look at a naïve thought experiment of the opposite case to help us understand what is going on a bit better. What would happen if Jesus stopped sustaining the waving of the quantum waves? Without a sustaining source of energy, the excitations in the quantum fields would die out. The waves would stop. The surface of the quantum fields would go back to being "flat." It would be just like what happens when we stop hitting a drum and it quickly becomes silent and still. What would become of the universe, if that happened? The particles, atoms, people, and galaxies would all suddenly cease to exist. Everything would go back into being only energy. In an instant, there would be nothing physically left in the universe.

Therefore, we should all be very thankful that Jesus is constantly sustaining all things, and that He is powerful enough, smart enough, and loves us enough to continually sustain us and the universe no matter what. Remember that God made a covenant with nature and keeps the laws fixed[12] as we talked about in the introduction, so we are in no danger of suddenly ceasing to exist.

Ponder the consequences of this for a moment. God is constantly sustaining and holding you together in the very depths of your nonphysical quantum waves. Inside each cell, inside each atom, inside each electron, God is sustaining the

---

[12] Jeremiah 33:25-26

waving and proper patterns of the quantum waves to keep you in existence every moment of every day. We can have no separate existence apart from God sustaining us.

God is inside your spirit, in the very core of your being, holding you in the most intimate way. You can't do anything apart from His sustaining power. You can't breathe, blink, or even just sit there without God holding you together. God is constantly sustaining you in every circumstance, trial, and joy in your life. God will never leave us or forsake us.[13] If He did, we would pop right out of existence physically and spiritually. We still exist, so God has not left us. God has not forsaken us. No matter what we have done or what we will do either good or bad, God will continually sustain us because He is good and He loves us and He keeps His covenant with nature and with us.

God also knows absolutely everything about you from the very depths of your spirit to the outward manifestation of your body that everyone else can see too. He knows your thoughts and emotions and every choice and motive. He knows more than just the number of hairs on your head.[14] He knows how many atoms, electrons, and quantum waves are in each hair. God is so intimate with us that we can't even begin to comprehend it. Emmanuel, God with us.

God's love is flowing in the deepest depths of our being: holding us, keeping us, and knowing us. That love sustains us and maintains us from the depths of our being to the outward manifestation of all things. The access point for

---

[13] Deuteronomy 31:6
[14] Psalm 139:1-18, Matthew 10:28-31, Luke 12:7

God's love and power to flow into our lives is in our spirits in the nonphysical quantum waves that builds us up. Intimacy is the currency of Heaven. Intimacy is the path that God's love, power, strength, joy, peace, etc. flows through to fill us and sustain or change everything around us.

Think about this: if God is holding everything together in the current configuration through the waving of the quantum waves, which make up everything, how easy is it for God to change the pattern of the quantum waves and make a new configuration manifest in the physical? The new configuration would look like a miraculous change took place in the physical realm. To put it another way: it is just as easy for God to do a miracle as not do one, since He is sustaining everything in one configuration or another. But, every change He makes is done through intimacy in the depths of the nonphysical quantum waves that make us up and is done in cooperation with us without forcing any changes on us.[15] God always works through intimacy and love.

We can all take a moment to thank God for sustaining us through every circumstance we have ever faced or ever will face. We can ponder how powerful, brilliant, creative, and

---

[15] There is nothing stopping God from doing any miracle He wants to. He is in complete control of everything, but He also gives us choices and chooses to respect all our choices and everyone else's choices in the past, present, and future. God also chooses to respect the laws of nature that He set in place. Many times, we have to deal with the consequences of our choices and/or someone else's choices. We also have to deal with the long term consequences of whether we, as all of humanity, have cooperated with nature or not throughout our history.

loving He is. God made the physical manifestation of our bodies out of nonphysical waves. Somehow, God found a way to wave nothing and make something. He is just that smart.

> *Romans 4:17b ESV, "in the presence of the God in whom he believed, who gives life to the dead and calls into existence the things that do not exist."*

The nonphysical eternal part of us is far more substantial and real than the temporary physical part. This physical realm that we can see and touch is not as solid and dependable as we would like to think, but God is solid and dependable. We can trust God and rely entirely on Him. We can all pray to become more aware of His Holy Spirit intimately holding us in the depths of our being and to become more aware of God's power to work in our lives and circumstances. We can all learn to trust God more and trust the world less.

Chapter 2
Higher Dimensional Space

Now that we understand how the physical universe is made out of some nonphysical substance, we can turn our attention to how the physical part of the universe fits into the rest of the universe. Science has discovered that there is a lot more to the universe than what we can see and observe with our physical instruments. We discussed the nonphysical quantum fields in the last chapter, but there is even more.

String theory tells us that there are at least 10 or 11 dimensions in the universe. We have the four dimensions (4D) of time, length, width, and height that we are used to in the physical part of the universe, but there are also at least six or seven more "something else" dimensions that are hidden inside the physical dimensions.

Each dimension is perpendicular to all the others. We see this when we look at a box. The length, width, and height are all perpendicular to each other. Each dimension is a direction of movement. On a line, which is one dimensional, one can only move forward or backwards. One direction; one dimension. Each dimension is also called a "Degree of Freedom." There is only one degree of freedom in a line. You are only free to move in one direction and you can only have line segments, rays, or the whole line contained within the line. The ability to do and be is very limited on a line. The line segments could be of any length, though. There are technically an infinite number of variations, but they all are still limited to the line.

When we add a dimension by going from a line to a plane, like a piece of paper, we add another direction of movement perpendicular to the first. Now, movement can happen in the forward and back direction and in the side-to-side direction. There are two directions; two dimensions; two degrees of freedom. There are a lot more ways to move around in a plane. Objects can move along a straight path or a curvy path, swirl around, or pass other objects. Many more types of objects can exist in a plane. There can be open and filled polygons, spirals, curves, and any number of other flat shapes. There is infinitely more ability to be and do in two degrees of freedom than in one. The infinity of options in one dimension have been multiplied by another infinity of options in two dimensions.

We can now add one more dimension and make a box. That brings us up to three dimensions; three directions; three degrees of freedom. Motion can happen in the forward and back direction, the side-to-side direction, and in the up and down direction or in any combination of the three directions.

There can be all kinds of complex solid or wire shapes and surfaces curving all around. Things can exist and move around in the wide variety of complex ways that we see in the world around us. We have multiplied the ability to be and do by another infinity by adding one more degree of freedom. There is an infinite amount of freedom in one dimension and an infinite amount of freedom in three dimensions, but they are very different types of infinities.

Then, we add six or seven more dimensions perpendicular to those three. How do we do that? What direction is perpendicular to length, width, and height all at the same time? The math is fairly straight forward,[1] but it's very hard to visualize. It is clear that any direction that is simultaneously perpendicular to all the three physical dimensions can't be pointed inside the physical dimensions. That direction has to go somewhere else, outside the physical dimensions.

As we add these six or more degrees of freedom, we are increasing the ability to be and do by infinity with each dimension. It is unfathomable what we could be and do with even one more degree of freedom, let alone if we had full access to all of the higher (nonphysical) dimensions. Take some time to think about it for a moment. Then, pause and ponder how much more freedom and ability must God have who created all the dimensions? Then, think about how

---

[1] The simplest math suited for working in higher dimensions is called linear algebra. It is the arithmetic of matrices. For each new dimension, we simply add more dimensions to the matrix. Anything higher than a three dimensional matrix is still hard to visualize, but computers have no problem working with them.

much freedom and ability He gives us access to in the unseen realm as the Holy Spirit leads us and teaches us? It is fun to think about the possibilities, but it's hard to know what is just our imagination and what is actually possible. Science is just beginning to explore the possibilities in the higher dimensions and just beginning to find experiments to determine what is actually out there. Stay tuned for exciting discoveries to come.

The whole universe contains the 4D physical space-time part that we are familiar with and the six or more higher nonphysical dimensions that we are just discovering. The quantum fields we discussed in the last chapter exist and wave in all the dimensions/directions whether physical or nonphysical. When the quantum waves all interfere with each other, they make total wave packets that are four-dimensional. The waving in the other nonphysical directions apparently cancels out as far as we can tell, so we can't measure it. This is what makes everything appear to be physical 4D space-time objects. The underlying quantum waves are waving in all of the possible dimensions, however.

It is important to note that the invisible/unseen realm, which the Bible refers to as the spiritual realm, is not some far distant place or in a parallel reality. The unseen dimensions are perpendicular to the seen dimensions. They are right here, right now, but in another direction that we can't usually perceive. Jesus told us that the "Kingdom of Heaven is at hand."[2] It is not far away and hard to reach.

---

[2] Matthew 3:2, 10:7, Mark 1:15, Luke 17:20-21

Some people have argued that the spiritual realm is like a parallel world much like a separate sheet of paper on top of the sheet of paper with our world in it. However, two parallel lines never meet. It would be impossible to ever get to Heaven or accomplish Jesus' prayer of "on Earth as it is in Heaven"[3] if Heaven was parallel to Earth, but that is not the case.

The unseen dimensions are very near to us. They are perpendicular to the seen dimensions, so they intersect at every point. Plus, the waves of the unseen quantum fields make up the atoms of our physical bodies. The unseen realm is very near to us. It is not hard to connect with the unseen realm. It is happening all the time whether we are aware of it or not. The unseen realm is not parallel. It is perpendicular.

The Whole Universe

Through astrophysics, we have determined that the edge of the observable physical universe is about 46.5 billion light years away at the present time. The whole universe is at least 78 billion light years across[4] and probably much, much bigger than that, but we have no way to measure how big the universe actually is. To help get a sense of scale, it takes light about 8.3 minutes to get to the Earth from the Sun. The Earth is about 93 million miles from the Sun on average and light traverses that distance in about 8 minutes! That is how

---

[3] Matthew 6:9-13, Luke 11:2-4

[4] N.J. Cornish, D.N. Spergel, G.D. Starkman, and E. Komatsu, Phys. Rev. Lett. 92, 201302 (2004). doi:10.1103/PhysRevLett.92.201302. 201302.

incredibly fast light is traveling. The next nearest star, Proxima Centauri, is about 4.24 light years away. That means it takes a little over 4 years for light to travel the almost 25 trillion miles to get here from the nearest star. In between, there is a whole lot of nothing (physical).[5]

Our Milky Way galaxy is about 100,000 light years across. Therefore, it takes about one hundred thousand years for light to get from one end of our galaxy to the other. When we look up at the night sky and see the other stars at the edge of the Milky Way, that light left some of those stars up to 100,000 years ago! It was somewhat less than that because the universe has been constantly expanding and so the stars were closer when the light left the other stars. There is a standard formula for figuring all that out, but that is beyond the scope of this book.[6] My point here is to help us begin to comprehend just how big the universe currently is.

As I stated above, our galaxy is about 100,000 light years across. The whole physical universe is at least 78 billion light years across in each of the three physical dimensions of length, width, and height. It's extremely hard for us to even begin to imagine the size of it, and it's growing bigger every day. Then, the Bible goes ahead and says that God holds the whole universe in the palm of His

---

[5] As we discussed in the last chapter, outer space is actually filled with "the vacuum", but is empty of anything physical except perhaps a few dust particles here and there.

[6] For other books that address the age and expansion of the universe from a scientific and theological perspective, check out the books *Why the Universe Is the Way It Is*, *A Matter of Days*, and *More Than a Theory* by astrophysicist Dr. Hugh Ross.

hand![7] Therefore, how big must God be? How big are your problems compared to God? Christ lives in you,[8] if you have let Him come into your heart. So, how big are your internal problems compared to God living in you? If you are in Christ,[9] everything has to go through Him to get to you. So, how big are your external problems compared to God? Let the truth of this sink in for a while. We would do well to keep everything in perspective.

So far, we have only looked at the three physical dimensions, not to mention however long time is. There are at least six more nonphysical dimensions in the entirety of the universe. So, how big is the whole of Creation? Science hasn't been able to figure out how big those other dimensions are yet. Some theories suggest that the nonphysical dimensions are very small, but we don't know exactly how small they are yet. If we say, for the sake of argument, that those six or more dimensions are as small as possible, we could get a naïve idea of the minimum size that the whole universe might be.

Let's say that those six or more other dimensions are just one unit long in each direction.[10] Everything in quantum

---

[7] Psalms 95:3-5, 102:25-27, Job 38:4-5, Isaiah 40:10-15

[8] Romans 8:9-11, 2 Corinthians 13:4-6, Galatians 4:19, Ephesians 1:13-14, 3:14-21, Colossians 1:27-29

[9] John 15:4-12, John 17:20-23, 1 Corinthians 1:30, Colossians 3:1-3, 2 Thessalonians 1:12

[10] The other six or more dimensions are nonphysical, so we can't measure them with a ruler in normal physical space units like meters. Therefore, we have to use other units. They still have a size and a space (called a Hilbert space) to move around in, but it is not a physical size.

physics seems to be quantized. That means that you can only have integer values of the smallest quantum units (called a "quantum"[11]). Therefore, there is a grid rather than a continuum and we can only put data points on the grid points, not just anywhere. Conveniently, this also makes it easier for us to visualize.

Let's start by looking at a dot on a line segment, which is one quantum long. On a grid, the dot can only be placed at 0 or 1 on the line segment. Therefore, we can fit two dots on a one-quantum line segment. In our minds, we can shrink the physical part of the universe down to a dot to begin to imagine the next higher dimension. If there was only one additional higher dimension and it was as small as possible, then we could potentially fit two of the physical universes in the whole universe. Inversely, we could argue that the physical part of universe was half of the whole universe. The other half would arguably be the nonphysical part of the universe. If the line segment was continuous, we could fit an infinite number of dots on the one unit long line segment. In that case, the physical part of the universe would be practically nothing compared to the rest of the universe.

If there were two higher dimensions, the quantized grid would look like a square. We can fit four dots on a unit square, as there can be dots at each of the four corners. For a unit box, there are eight corners, so we can fit eight dots on a

---

[11] The quantized units can be of many different types. Energy and momentum are the most common things that we measure and are always quantized in the microscopic world. We can have a quantum of energy or a quantum of momentum, which are fundamentally different from each other.

unit box. As we keep adding dimensions that are one unit long, we multiply the number of corners by 2 each time. Thus, for six higher dimensions, we have 64 corners. There could be even more than that with each higher dimension that we discover. With at least six higher dimensions that are as small as possible, we could theoretically fit 64 dots the size of the physical part of the universe into the whole universe.

Remember that each one of those dots is a bubble with a diameter of at least 78 billion light years or more. The other 63 dots of the same immense size would be the nonphysical part of the universe in this minimalistic argument. In other words, the unseen realm should be at least 63 times the size of the seen realm, and that's just the 'as small as possible' size of the unseen realm in our naïve thought experiment. It is probably much bigger than that.

Let's ponder for a bit how big the nonphysical (spiritual) part of the universe might be! Let the sheer size of the unseen realm sink in for a moment. How much is there yet to explore in the unseen realm that we haven't even begun to scratch the surface of? Then, ponder how little the physical part of the universe is relative to the whole universe. In this naïve argument, the seen realm is at the most, 1/64 (about 1.5%) of the whole of Creation and most likely much, much smaller than that. There is so much more to the universe than we can see. The unseen realm is unimaginably bigger than the seen realm. Plus, we have all those infinities of freedom to be and to do as we begin to explore the unseen dimensions also!

Now, the other dimensions are probably not as small as possible and there may be more than six other dimensions, so the percentage of the physical part is probably much, much lower than 1.5%. Also, if the other dimensions are continuous rather than quantized, the seen realm is practically nothing compared to the whole. In this extremely simplistic argument, the unseen realm is at least 98.5% of everything in the universe. More than likely, it is much closer to almost 100%. We have no idea what the numbers actually are, so don't quote me on this.

Where do we spend all of our time focusing? Most of us spend most of our time focusing on the one tiny dot of the physical realm, so our minds blow that dot out of proportion while we largely ignore the immensity of the nonphysical realm. The physical universe is unbelievably huge and magnificent, but there is so much more to the rest of Creation! We have only just begun to scratch the surface of exploring the nonphysical/unseen realm. I can't wait to see what we discover as we continue to explore there.

Observations of the Higher Dimensions

The question is: how do we explore the unseen realm when we can't directly observe it? Let's look at an example to help us get a better grid for how we can indirectly observe the unseen realm. Take a look at Figure 6 and stare at it for a moment and observe whether the dotted line is in the front or in the back. Keep staring at it for a while and you should observe that the dotted line shifts back and forth between the front and the back. That's your brain rotating the box

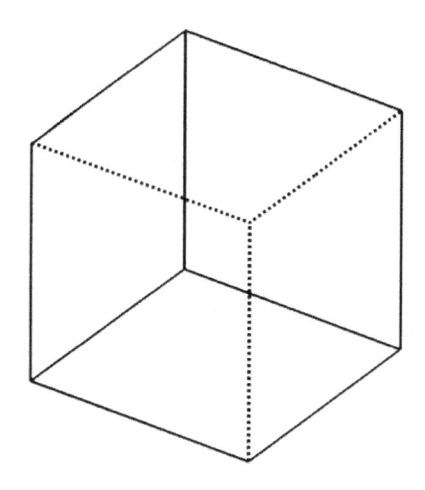

Figure 6: Is the dotted line in the front or back?

through the next dimension! A real wire box couldn't shift straight through the other wires like that, but with access to one more dimension, it could. Your brain can almost handle thinking about one more dimension. So, there is hope for eventually being able to think of some experiments to observe other dimensions too.

Getting back to the question at hand, what have you observed in Figure 6? Is the dotted line in the front or in the back? In the front, in the back, both, and neither are all acceptable and correct answers. This example demonstrates that we have to be careful about how we ask our experimental questions or else we will get nonsensical answers.

The drawing is technically a two dimensional flat object that doesn't have a front or back, so we can argue that the dotted line is neither in the front nor in the back. Therefore asking the question about the front or back is nonsensical.

59

However, we still always observe it either in the front or in the back and it never actually looks like a flat object to us. Therefore, we can just as easily argue that it is a picture of a three dimensional object which does have a front and a back to it, so we can ask about that. There is no way for us to tell from our observations if the "true" answer is always changing between front and back; both front and back; or neither front or back.

About half the time, we observe that the dotted line is in the front. The other half of the time, we observe that the dotted line is in the back. Therefore, when we observe the dotted line in the front, it is correct to say that it is. The same is true when we observe that the dotted line is in the back.

However, those individual observations don't tell the whole story. The picture with the dotted line in front looks identical to the picture with the dotted line in the back, and the two pictures could be superimposed on each other, so we can't distinguish them. We can say that there is a 50/50 probability distribution of observing the dotted line in the front or in the back. We have a distribution of possible answers that each has a certain probability of being observed the next time we look at the drawing.

This is the case in our quantum experiments, too. In quantum physics lingo, we say that the dotted line is in an equal quantum superposition of being in the front and the back.[12] It is equally both at the same time, but we can only

---

[12] For the quantum physics/math junkies out there, the actual formula for this quantum superposition with a 50/50 probability split is $\Psi = (|Front\rangle + |Back\rangle)/\sqrt{2}$

observe one answer at a time because that is the only way for the object to be a real three dimensional thing that we can have a picture of at any given time.

When we do our experiments, we make an observation and get one of the possible answers.[13] Then, we repeat the experiment many, many times and get a different answer from the set of possible answers each time. After we get enough data, we can mathematically figure out what the probability distribution of each possible answer is. Finally, we can reconstruct the superposition and figure out what the full state of the object is beyond what we can measure.

We can think of it like taking a large number of two-dimensional images or shadows of a three-dimensional object from all different angles and trying to reconstruct the full object from all the flat shadow pictures. We can imagine that fairly easily because we are used to working with 3D objects. But, if we were 2D creatures trying to reconstruct a 3D object that no one had ever seen before, it would be very confusing and there would be tons of heated debate about it. It is the same for us when we try to take 4D (space-time) measurements of higher dimensional quantum particles (strings).

Another question we can ask is this: is the wire box in the picture really changing every time we observe it differently, or is it always the same and it is just what we are able to observe that is changing? It's easy to understand that the wire box isn't actually changing from front to back because we know the drawing on the paper is static. We are

---

[13] Each possible answer is called an "Eigenstate" in physics.

seeing a different piece of the puzzle every time, but the puzzle itself isn't changing. However, when our limited quantum measurements give us different answers each time, somehow we think the objects themselves are spontaneously changing in impossible ways, but it is just our limited ability to observe the fullness of the objects that causes the changes in our observations. We can only see one aspect of the full object each time we observe it. We need to keep this in mind as we are trying to interpret the data properly.

Optical Illusions

Let's look for a moment at what is happening inside our brains when we observe the dotted line as being in the front or the back. Our brains are used to seeing 3D objects all the time. When we see a drawing that looks like a 3D box, our brains automatically assume that it is a 3D box, but there isn't enough information for our brains to guess the orientation of the box accurately. Sometimes, our brains guess that the dotted line is in the front and other times our brains guess that it is in the back. Our brains are constantly interpreting the visual data and making a guess. That is why the drawing seems to switch back and forth.

Our brains are always doing this with everything we see. The outer electrons in the atoms on the surfaces of all the objects around us are giving off light or reflecting light, which at a quantum level is the same thing – it's just an electron sending out a photon of light regardless of where the energy came from. Then, the electrons in the retinas of our eyes absorb the photons from the objects and send an electrical signal down the neural pathways to our brains. The visual cortex in our brains then interprets that electrical signal as a color and an intensity and puts that together with all the other electrical signals to make a picture in our imagination.

There are a couple things to note about this process. First, our brains can't tell the difference between pictures we imagine and pictures we see. The brain reacts and processes them the same way. Our bodies follow suit and react to them the same way, too. We need to be careful about what we allow ourselves to imagine and what we spend time thinking about. The Bible advises us[14] to think about good things because it will benefit our life and our health. Modern neuroscience is saying the same thing too. I won't go into any more detail about that here, as there are several other good books on the subject by experts in that field.[15]

Second, the entire process of "seeing" is not physical. The electrons that send and receive the photons are orbiting the nucleus in a standing wave pattern. Remember that electrons are really wave packets of rapidly waving non-physical quantum fields, so they aren't really physical when they are being wave-like. The photons are also wave packets of non-physical electromagnetic waves. The electrical current in your nervous system is made out of electrons traveling along the circuit in a more wave-like (less

---

[14] Proverbs 4:23, 23:19, Psalms 139:23-24, Matthew 12:35, Romans 12:2, 2 Corinthians 10:3-6, Philippians 4:8

[15] For more information about the science of our thoughts and how they affect our bodies, I recommend the book, *Switch on Your Brain* by neuroscientist Dr. Caroline Leaf.

localized/physical) way. Finally, the brain makes a picture of the object in our imagination, which is arguably not physical.

Therefore, "seeing" isn't really a physical process. As we discussed in the last chapter, "touching" isn't really a physical process either. It is just the electromagnetic repulsion between the electrons on the outside of our skin and whatever object we are touching. The brain then interprets the push back from the electromagnetic repulsion as the existence of an object. In fact, all of our senses operate through similar non-physical mechanisms either through electromagnetism or through quantum chemistry.[16] We have to put the data from multiple senses together to reassure ourselves that the object is actually there and not just in our imagination. When we all see, hear, and touch the same things in the same way, we come to a consensus about what is real. We can then relax and go on about our lives.

Ultimately, we are all just making assumptions and guesses about what we are seeing, hearing, and touching. We have amassed so much experience in the world throughout our lives that we can operate very confidently about our educated guesses, though. The chair has always held us up, so there is no reason to even think about it now. We just sit down and the chair holds us up. In the case of the wire box drawing in Figure 6, we have seen and touched so many

---

[16] At a fundamental level, chemical interactions operate through electromagnetic attraction and repulsion, too, so pretty much everything that happens on a macroscopic level is governed by electricity and magnetism.

boxes, that our brain automatically sees a box and never sees a hexagon with some strategically placed internal lines.

This is technically just an optical illusion. That's how all optical illusions work. They force our brain to reference something we have seen before. Our brain can't help but make the designated assumption and put that previous image up on the screen in our imagination. It's practically impossible to see the original image for what is actually is – just a bunch of carefully laid out lines and shapes.

My point is that our brains are taking the 2D data in the drawing and putting it in the closest 3D box from our mental library that it can find, and our brains always do this. When we talk about the higher dimensions and non-physical data, the brain also takes those signals, picks the closest 4D (space-time) experience we have had, and identifies it as that. We are always interpreting everything through a 4D lens. When we do that, we don't see the full picture. We only see one facet of it. We are also seeing a distorted picture since we had to squish the original into the closest box. There aren't any other options really. That is how our brains work. The only thing we can do is to gain more experience with more variety, so we can have a better grid for all kinds of data.

We need to be aware that this is happening so we can have an ample amount of humility and healthy skepticism about what we are sensing. Our brains and our eyes, ears, etc. are not very good or reliable scientific instruments. They should not be trusted implicitly. There is no way for us to actually know if the electrical signals that our brains are interpreting as the world around us are really real or if they are just our imagination.

Only God knows what is really real and what is actually true. He exists outside of the universe and isn't subject to the limitations of how our brains work. He isn't stuck inside a 4D worldview. We can trust God, but we can't trust our own perception. I hope I have convinced you that the world around us isn't as solid and dependable as we thought it was. However, God is a constant, unchanging solid rock that never lies,[17] and God has everything under His control. He can be trusted completely and without question. He loves us and wants what is best for us.[18] God wants to connect with us intimately and work with us in all our circumstances. He will guide us into all truth[19] as we let Him teach us and show us what reality actually is. All we have to do is ask Him to teach us and guide us and He will.

I mentioned before that our best scientific instruments are still four-dimensional and can only measure 4D data. Similar to our brains, they are also only able to measure certain aspects of the higher dimensional quantum particles (strings) during each run of an experiment. Our physical experiments are inherently limited, but until our brains can think outside the 4D box and come up with higher

---

[17] Numbers 23:19, 1 Samuel 15:29, Psalms 33:11, Psalms 102:25-27, 110:4, Isaiah 46:9-10, 54:10, 55:8-13, Malachi 3:6, Romans 11:29, Hebrews 6:17-20, Hebrews 13:8, James 1:17

[18] Exodus 34:6-7, Deuteronomy 7:6-9, 23:5, Jeremiah 31:3, John 16:27, Romans 8:28, Ephesians 2:4-9, Titus 3:4-7, 1 John 4:7-11, 16-19

[19] John 14:26, 16:13, 1 Corinthians 2:9-16, 1 John 2:27

dimensional instruments, we have to do our best with what we have.

Even with the limitations of our equipment and experiments, we have still managed to make some discoveries about the higher dimensions and the non-physical part of the universe as we have been discussing so far in these two chapters. We can reconstruct the higher dimensional superposition by making lots of measurements about each facet of the system we are measuring and thereby gather some information about the fullness of the system. As we develop better and better experiments and instruments, I'm sure that we will continue to discover much more.

Chapter 3
Time & Eternity

Time is another dimension like all the others. On a quantum scale, there is no way to differentiate between time and space. It is just another variable in our equations the same as all the rest. On a macroscopic (everyday life) scale, it is clear that time and space are very different; however, the quantum mathematical models are unable to fully account for that difference. We all know that time only moves in one direction, from past to future, but we don't know exactly why yet.

Historically, scientists have described time as a sequence of events linked by causality. Causality is a fancy word for the link between the reason some event or change happened (the cause) and the event or change itself (the effect). Cause and effect is clearly one directional. In our experience, something causes a change to happen and not the other way around. The cause makes the effect happen after the cause happened, and the effect never runs backwards and makes the cause happen first.

However, one effect can become a cause for another effect. For example, each person exists because of the choices that their parents made. The parents' actions are the cause and the baby is the effect. The baby can then grow up and cause another baby to be born. This link of cause and effect has gone on from the first humans until today and will continue as long as there are people. We mark out that sequence of generations with time. That sequence always seems to move forward in one direction.

That is also how the universe has developed from the creation until now and through to the end. There has been a long sequence of events starting with the first cause. It propagated forward causing changes in the universe's expansion and development, which then caused other changes. Those changes cause even more changes, and so on for all of time. Time is what we use to measure the sequence of cause and effect as the whole universal system changes and develops.

Marking out time with a clock or a calendar allows us to measure how things change as the sequence of cause and effect develops and grows. Each moment in time marks the state of the whole universal system at that moment, like each frame in a movie reel. Then, the state of some little thing changes and we have the next moment in time, the next frame in the movie of history. The state of the physical universe and everything in it is constantly changing in many tiny ways and time is constantly marching forward.

In the nonphysical/unseen/spiritual part of the universe, we see a very different situation regarding time. Let's look at what the Bible has to say and compare that with what science says.

> *2 Corinthians 4:18, "So we fix our eyes not on what is seen, but on what is unseen, since what is seen is temporary, but what is unseen is eternal."*

This Bible verse is telling us about the characteristics of the seen and unseen realms as they relate to time. The verse says that the seen realm (the 4D space-time that we can see and observe) has the characteristic of being temporary and the unseen realm (everything else that we can't see directly) has the characteristic of being eternal. We are also being instructed to focus our attention on the unseen realm confirming what we discussed in the last chapter on higher dimensions.

What does it mean to be temporary or eternal? Temporary means that a system (some group of objects) is changing quickly and doesn't stay in one state or configuration for very long. The changes in systems that are temporary can be measured by time. Remember that time measures change, and there is a lot of change in temporary systems.

In fact, the word "temporary" is derived from the word for time. Systems that are temporary are temporal; that is, they are described by time and exist inside the dimension of time. We can say that temporary systems are bound by time or are strongly influenced by time. Time matters a lot to a temporary system. The side effect of this is that there can only be changes in the state of something inside the cause and effect process of time.

Eternal systems, on the other hand, remain forever without changing. If something eternal changed its state, it would become temporary, wouldn't it? Eternal systems do not change their state. The state or configuration of the system is locked in, and it can't change at all. Therefore, we cannot use time to measure anything about an eternal system. Time measures change and in eternal systems, there is no change to measure. Eternal systems are not temporal. Eternal systems do not care about time and are not influenced or bound by time. Once time becomes an irrelevant variable, changes in the state of a system down to the most minute level are no longer possible.

We see from 2 Corinthians 4:18 that the seen realm (our 4D physical world) is temporary. That agrees with what we see and know from our normal lives. That is why we describe our normal experiences as 4D – time, length, width, and height. On the other hand, the verse also says that the unseen realm (containing the other six or more dimensions and the quantum fields[1]) is eternal and not influenced, described, or measured by time.

We may be tempted to think that since nothing can change in a timeless system that everything would just stop

---

[1] The waves in the quantum fields are constantly oscillating. The total wave patterns (wave packets) make up the physical particles, which change states frequently, but, the underlying unseen quantum fields themselves are constant and unchanging, and thus they are eternal.

or freeze as we leave the seen realm and go into the unseen realm, but this is not the case. In quantum physics, a system where time becomes irrelevant is called "adiabatic."[2] One interesting thing about adiabatic systems is that the state of the system itself can still evolve very slowly and smoothly. However, any particle stuck in an adiabatic state can't change to another state because there are no quantum fluctuations.

Quantum fluctuations are tiny rapid chaotic wiggles in the quantum fields that allow quantum particles to change their state from one configuration to another. Without fluctuations, no quantum particle could change its state. The quantum particles (and thus everything made out of them including you and me) are stuck in whatever state they are in forever.

For example, particles cannot jump from one energy level to another without quantum fluctuations giving them a little wiggle to get them started. They are stuck in their energy level rut and need a little boost to get over the edge of the rut. Without that little boost, the particles are stuck in the rut forever.

---

[2] An adiabatic process in quantum physics is very different from the use of that term in thermodynamics. In quantum physics, an adiabatic process happens sufficiently slowly and time becomes an irrelevant variable. This usage is more similar to the term "quasi-static" in thermodynamics. In thermodynamics, adiabatic processes are ones where the system is isolated from the environment in such a way that no heat or matter is transferred or lost. In either case, certain elements of the system remain constant in the initial state throughout the process.

We can only have quantum fluctuations and the associated rapid changes in a system where there is time. In a timeless system, there is no ability to make quick changes and thus no quantum fluctuations and thus no jumping between states. Everything happens smoothly and continuously in a timeless system.

The rut that some particle is in can slowly curve along, but the particle cannot jump over to another rut. The particles follow the evolution of the state in perfect synchronization. Rather than incorrectly picturing freezing the state, think of it more like being in a train car that is moving along a track, and there is no way to jump into another car on some other track. Anything in a timeless system is stuck in whatever train car it is in, with whatever else is in there, forever. Nothing can get in or out.

We have the physical part of the universe that contains time and physical space where changing our state[3] is possible, and we also have the set of nonphysical dimensions in the universe which doesn't contain a time dimension. Therefore, the eternal state of everything in the unseen realm is fixed. If you are getting lost in all this science-y lingo, let me boil it down to one thought: the Bible and science agree that physical things are temporary and change frequently and that spiritual things are eternal and don't change.

Don't think that we are losing anything by moving beyond time, however. In the higher dimensions, things do

---

[3] Our "state" could encompass any or all of the state of our physical body and circumstances, our mental and emotional state, and/or our spiritual state of being.

not change in a time-like way as we would expect, but that doesn't mean everything is static. Remember that we have infinitely more freedom to be and do in the higher dimensions and there is an unimaginably huge amount of nonphysical "space" to move around in. We can't even fathom the possibilities. Losing time isn't much of a loss. However, it may be hard to fathom how much more we can do without the restrictions of time.

Higher dimensional systems are not governed by time. In an eternal system, time no longer has mastery over us. There is so much more freedom in the timeless unseen part of the universe for us to explore and understand.

Eternal Theology

Since time doesn't matter in an eternal system, we can no longer use any time-like words to describe an eternal system such as Heaven. We can't say "before" and "after" and "when" anymore. Those words don't make any sense in a system that doesn't change. We can't have a sequence of events in a timeless system either.

This has a huge impact on our theology. We run into so many problems because we interpret the description of what exists in Heaven as though those things are events occurring inside time and physical space. Then, we forcibly try to turn them into physical things and events that fit into a time line, but they are not. They are higher dimensional spiritual things that are eternal. They simply exist. We must look at all the descriptions of Heavenly things as eternal realities that are always true rather than looking at them as temporary events and physical objects.

It is natural for us to squeeze everything into time and space since all of our experience comes from inside time. It's very difficult to understand anything else. Our brains are bound by time, and they automatically shove any spiritual experiences we have or read about into the nearest time-like box from our normal 4D life. All spiritual data is naturally processed by the brain in a sequential, time-like way. The brain can't do anything else, but that doesn't mean the original spiritual data had anything to do with time or was sequential in any way.

It is also very hard to describe eternal systems to others verbally or in writing, since we have very few words to describe systems where time is irrelevant. And, we certainly don't have any higher dimensional words. Therefore, we have to be very careful in how we interpret the Scriptures or experiences that involve timeless systems keeping in mind the differences and difficulties.

The people in the Bible who saw visions and had spiritual experiences did their best, under the inspiration of the Holy Spirit, to describe their timeless nonphysical experiences with mere human words. Their brains had the same problem our brains have in squeezing the nonphysical, timeless Heavenly experiences into physical time-like words and pictures. The Holy Spirit certainly helped them do the best job possible with that interpretation to make sure the description was the best one possible. However, no physical

4D words could possibly contain the fullness of the higher dimensional spiritual communication from God.

We have to keep this in mind as we are reading the physical words on the pages of the Bible. We have to remember that Jesus Himself is the fullness of the Word of God.[4] He is way beyond our little 4D words. If we just read the words on the pages of the Bible with our minds that are stuck in our 4D worldview, we will be missing all of the spiritual components of what the Bible is talking about. When we do that, we reduce the higher dimensional, nonphysical, eternal realities to temporary, physical, lower dimensional shadows.[5]

If we only look at the shadow with our minds, we are prone to making many assumptions, and we will end up with many misunderstandings. We then get into all kinds of arguments with each other about what the Bible is really saying, and we find all sorts of things that seem like contradictions. Scholars spend their whole lives trying to make sense out of the Bible with their minds and coming up with all kinds of complex theology to try to fit it into a 4D world system. The Bible, however, is speaking about a higher dimensional, nonphysical reality. All sorts of things are possible in the higher dimensions that would be impossible in our 4D physical world. Complex things become incredibly simple in higher dimensions. If we only look at the physical, we are sure to misunderstand much, if not all of the Bible.

---

[4] John 1:1, 14, Revelation 19:13
[5] Colossians 2:17, Hebrews 8:1-6, 9:23-28, 10:1-2

We need to allow Jesus through the Holy Spirit to read the words in the Bible to us through our personal communication with Him. When the Holy Spirit reads the Bible to us, He speaks with the fullness of all the spiritual meaning beyond the mere 4D words on the page. Only when God's spiritual words combine with the physical words on the page will the fullness of the spiritual truths in the Bible communicate properly to our spirits. Only God knows how to read and interpret the Bible properly. Open up your heart and ask Him to read it to you.

Eternally Now

The simplest way to think about the timeless zone of the universe is to remember that it is always, eternally now in that zone. There is no past or future, only the present.[6] It is always now in Heaven because Heaven exists in an eternal, timeless zone. That eternal reality, that "eternal now" affects what happens inside the timeline of human history and intersects with the timeline in various ways at various points. The "eternal now" presses into our timeline at every point perpendicularly and brings our constantly changing temporary reality into alignment with the eternal reality.

We can imagine that our eternal state is like a constant force pulling on us. When a constant force, like gravity, pulls on an object, the object moves towards the source faster and faster. When we drop a ball, it starts out at rest and then falls

---

[6] Psalms 90:1-4, 102:24-28, Isaiah 41:4, Malachi 3:6, John 8:58, James 1:17, Hebrews 4:7, 13:8, Revelation 1:17-18

faster and faster. The more time gravity has had to pull on the ball, the faster it will fall and the closer it will get to the source. In the same way, our eternal reality pulls on us to align us with that state throughout our lifetimes.

The longer we spend inside the timeline, the more we grow and mature into being what we are like in our eternal reality. The connection and cooperation we have here and now with our eternal reality opens up more influence from that eternal reality, which then brings about even more connection and cooperation in our lives. It is an endless spiraling towards our eternal state. That is how acceleration, growth, and maturity happen.

Of course, other things can happen to interrupt the process and pull us in other directions too. That is why we can sometimes "backslide" or go in many different directions during different stages in our lives, but God is always drawing us toward becoming who He created us to be. Likewise, the enemy is always dragging us toward becoming what the enemy wants us to be, but God is stronger.

We get to choose which force to open ourselves up to in each moment of our lives. Our openness allows that force to pull on us and move us closer to that way of thinking, feeling, and acting, whether good or bad. The more we choose God's eternal state or the enemy's eternal state, the faster we will move towards ending up in one state or the other. It is always our choice. In eternity, we will be the best version of ourselves or the worst version of ourselves. It is up to us to choose which one we will be.

In eternity, Christians have been fully perfected in Christ and are completely unified with Him.[7] As we grow and mature into being more Christ-like during our lives, we are accessing more of the eternal now reality and pulling that perfected in Christ version of ourselves into the timeline. From our time bound perspective, it looks like we are growing more like Christ. However, from an eternal perspective, the ultimate reality of who we always are in Christ and the reality of what He did for us on the Cross is manifesting more and more into the timeline as it progresses along. That ultimate reality manifests more and more as we become more synchronized with our eternal reality. We grow and mature as we bring more of the now in Heaven into our now on earth. As we move forward in time, we are better able to do that. We become more and more free from being tossed about by the winds and waves[8] of the temporary and become more secure in the eternal unchanging rock of Christ Jesus.[9]

God shows us the reality that He is always in the present when He talks about Himself and how He sees us.

> *Exodus 3:14, "God said to Moses, "I AM WHO I AM. This is what you are to say to the Israelites: 'I AM has sent me to you.' ""*

---

[7] Ephesians 1:7-14, 4:11-16, 5:25-27, Colossians 2:9-10, Colossians 3:14, Hebrews 10:1-2, 10:14, 12:22-24, Revelation 19:6-8

[8] Ephesians 4:11-16, James 1:5-8

[9] Exodus 17:6, 2 Samuel 22:2-3, 22:32-33, 22:47, Psalms 18:2, 18:31-32, 18:46, 62:2, 62:5-8, 95:1, Matthew 7:24-27, Luke 6:47-49, 1 Corinthians 10:1-4

God is the 'I AM.' He always is. We have a past and a future, a beginning and an end, but God just is. God is always present.

> *Luke 20:37-38, "But in the account of the burning bush, even Moses showed that the dead rise, for he calls the Lord 'the God of Abraham, and the God of Isaac, and the God of Jacob.' He is not the God of the dead, but of the living, for to him all are alive."*

Jesus says that everyone is presently alive from God's perspective in Heaven.[10] He sees the entire timeline of history at once without being bound by it, so He can presently interact with everyone at any point in history all at once. Everyone is alive to God. He is the God of the living and not the dead.

That means that God can interact with us at every point in our history: past, present, and future. Think about an old movie reel containing the whole timeline of history. The people in the movie are stuck in the film moving along in one direction as each frame advances. They don't know the future and can't go back to the past. However, from Heaven's perspective, the whole movie is sitting there completed and God can look at any and every frame without concerning Himself with time or sequence. God knows the beginning and the end and everything in between.

God can help us and work miracles in our lives at any point in our timeline. God is able to forgive our past and

---

[10] John 8:58

future sins because Jesus is there at all points in time. They are all present for Him. God can heal our painful memories and restore broken relationships because He is present when they were broken and present when they are restored. Our God is God over time. He is everywhere and every-when and beyond. There is nowhere and no-when we can go to hide from Him.[11]

God is actively loving us at every point in our timeline from conception until death and beyond into eternity. God is also constantly working to line us up and bring us into unity with the fullness of how He designed us to be in eternity. We get to choose to cooperate with Him to become the best version of ourselves. Time will no longer be our master as we allow Christ in us to manifest His timeless reality in our lives and bring Heaven's reality to Earth now.

---

[11] Psalm 139

Chapter 4
Quantum Leaping

We talked in Chapter 1 about how God is sustaining everything in the universe through the waving of the nonphysical quantum fields. The waves of the quantum force fields combine together to make quantum particles, which make atoms and bigger objects. God's intimate control over the quantum waves makes it very easy for Him to manipulate the configuration of all the particles, atoms, and everything else in the universe.

We talked about how God can easily change the configuration of the quantum waves to change the visible states of the things we can see to do miracles without violating any of the laws of nature. There are also other ways which God can change the configuration of the particles and larger objects in the universe to perform miracles. We will explore some of those ways in this chapter.

Humans also have the ability to manipulate the quantum particles, and larger objects, by understating the rules and using the forces of nature. This is how we make tools, machines, and technology. When we understand how forces work, we can make objects move. For example, we use forces to move objects with levers, screws, and many other machines. When we understand how electricity and magnetism work, we can make electric circuits and other devices. The more we have come to understand the fundamental forces of nature, the more we can make new tools and devices that drive the technological advances in our world today and improve the lives of everyone.

Forces of Nature

The forces in nature are the Electric, Magnetic, Strong, Weak, and Gravity forces. These are all the forces that we have discovered so far. There are no other fundamental forces. All the other forces that we encounter in our daily lives like pressure, friction, and tension are all combinations of the fundamental forces, primarily the electromagnetic and gravitational forces. The strong and weak forces only operate inside the atoms, so we won't talk about them here. We will focus on the forces we are familiar with because they are operating in our visible world and they are easier to understand.

The main thing that we need to understand about forces is that they move energy around. For example, the force from the wind blowing across the surface of the ocean creates waves on the surface of the ocean. The energy in the wind gets transferred into the energy in the ocean waves. Then, the ocean waves carry that energy until it hits something else. The ocean waves will move buoys up and down and carry boats and surfers along with the waves. The waves will move the sand on the shore back and forth in sync with the wave.

All waves are generated by forces imparting energy to them. When the energy in the wave interacts with some other object, it will change the state of that object to line up with the movement of the source. Waves, therefore, help distant objects synchronize with each other and come into unison with each other. An object's state could be how much energy it has, how fast it is moving or vibrating, or where it is located. All these things will be influenced by the energy of an incoming wave.

When we are trying to determine how some object will be affected by all of the complex forces acting on it, we combine all the forces into an "energy potential field" for each type of force. For example, a falling magnet will have an energy potential field for the gravity force, and it will have another one for the electromagnetic force from other nearby metals, magnets, or currents as well as the Earth's magnetic field. The combination of all these forces will determine how the magnet moves, but we won't get into all the complicated math of that.

The energy potential is like a roller coaster track. In a roller coaster, the engineers design the track so that the car can move around in a specified pattern using only the force of gravity. The car, or particle in our case, can only go as

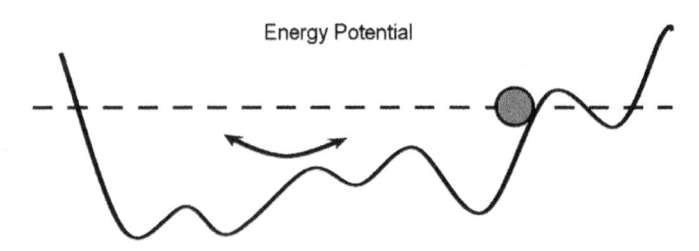

Figure 7: Schematic of a gravitational energy potential for a ball rolling in a curvy bowl.

high as its initial energy lets it. All the actions of a particle can be determined by the energy potential, the amount of energy it has, and the amount of momentum (mass, speed, and direction) it has. We can use the different forces to make a potential that looks like almost anything we want, just like the roller coaster designer. Thereby, we can make the quantum particles move in any number of ways.

Let's look at the gravitational energy potential for a ball in a curvy bowl in order to help us understand how this works (see Figure 7). If we put a ball in a frictionless bowl and let go, it will start rolling back and forth. It will go down one side and up the other side of the bowl to reach the same height as it started with. If there is no friction to slow it down, the ball will keep rolling back and forth forever always reaching the same height.

In the quantum world, there are no dissipative forces like friction, so everything keeps whatever energy it has to start with unless it gives it to something else. That is law of energy conservation, which says that energy is not lost or gained in a closed system. The energy can change forms from one type of force or movement to another, but all the energy stays in the system in one form or another.

If we start the ball out from a higher spot, it will be able to access more of the bowl/energy potential because it has more energy when it is higher up. In the visible world, where classical mechanics is valid, a ball would not be able to roll over a hill that was higher than its energy level. Thus, the ball in Figure 7 could roll anywhere below the dashed line, but we would never find the ball in the rightmost valley because it couldn't get over the barrier of the hill. We say that the ball is energetically forbidden to go into the rightmost valley.

Quantum Tunneling

Strangely, in the quantum world, we sometimes find the ball in the rightmost valley, even though that should be impossible. This surprising effect is called "Quantum Tunneling" because the quantum particles seem to tunnel through the barrier to get to the other side. The particles do not have enough energy to go over the top of the barrier, so they had to get to the other side in some other way.

How does that happen? When this phenomenon was first discovered, people came up will all kinds of crazy theories about how it might work, but it turns out that the explanation is fairly simple. It isn't as crazy as it appears at first glance. The main thing we need to remember is that quantum particles are wave packets. The wave-like properties of the quantum particles removes almost all of the craziness in quantum physics, and it does in this case too.

Individual Waves

Interference (3 Waves)

Wave Packet (Many Waves)

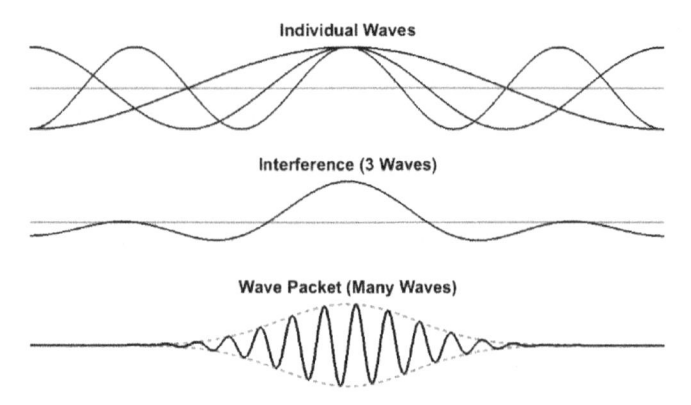

Figure 8: Wave interference adds up to make a wave packet.

Let's look at a wave packet again to help us see how it makes seemingly impossible things possible (see Figure 8). The quantum particles, like electrons and photons, are made out of a huge number of component quantum waves that are interfering with each other to make a little ball-like packet. The total wave pattern of the wave packet has a large amplitude in the middle and quickly dies off in the tails as the oscillations get farther from the center. Notice, however, that the amplitude never actually gets to zero. There is always a little bit of waving going on even infinitely far away from the center. It is this little bit of waving in the tails that allows for quantum tunneling to occur.

Recall from Chapter 1 that we can only measure the total wave pattern, and we currently have no way to measure the component quantum waves. We can also only measure one position for the particle at a time. We have to do many repeated experiments and record many locations for the quantum particle in order to reconstruct what the wave pattern really is. Where the amplitude of the quantum waves

Quantum Tunneling

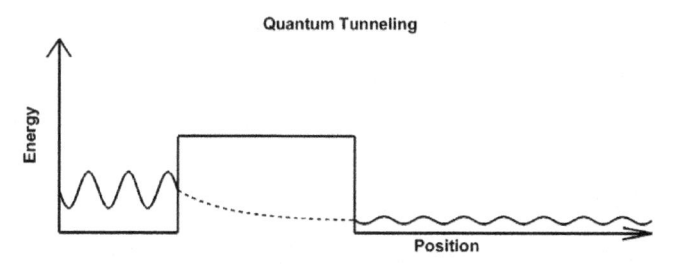

Figure 9: A particle in an energy well. Some of the quantum waves leak out onto the other side of the barrier.

is large, we will measure the particle there more often. Where the amplitude of the quantum waves is small, we will measure the particle there rarely. How big the oscillations in the quantum waves are directly relates to where we find the quantum particle when we do our experiments.

Figure 9 shows a simple energy potential of a particle in a well with a small barrier on one side. In the visible world, a particle would simply bounce back and forth inside the well at whatever height corresponded to its energy level. However, in the quantum world, the underlying waves of the quantum particle extend out through the barrier to the other side. The size of the waves drops dramatically as it "tunnels" through the barrier. As a loose analogy, we can think of it as though the waves are losing energy trying to get through the energy barrier. A higher or wider barrier will make the waves on the other side lose more energy than a short or narrow barrier. We can't see what is actually happening inside the barrier, though. Also, the total energy is still conserved, so the analogy isn't perfect.

Once the tails of waves get to the other side, we can start to observe what happens again. The oscillations in the tails on the other side of the barrier have a small amplitude, and so we will only measure the particle there rarely. But, rarely is more than never! Most of the time, we find the particle inside the well where it belongs, but every now and then, we find the particle somewhere else where it wouldn't be allowed in classical mechanics. Thus, the wave-like nature of the quantum particles allows them to go to places that should be impossible to access in the visible world.

This phenomenon has been put to good use in the Tunneling Electron Microscope, which can take detailed pictures of tiny dust mites, nano-circuits, and the individual atoms on the surface of materials. There are many amazing pictures that were taken with a Tunneling Electron Microscope on the internet, if you want to look them up.

Quantum Leaping

Quantum leaping is another strange phenomenon in quantum physics that sounds crazy on the surface, but isn't. Quantum leaping is the phenomenon responsible for all the light that we see around us. The electrons in every atom are participating in this phenomenon all the time.

Inside each atom, there are many electrons orbiting the nucleus in complex three-dimensional orbits. These orbits are very strictly defined. The electrons aren't allowed to be just anywhere. They have to stay within their allowed orbits. It is kind of like our solar system where each of the planets is at a certain average distance from the sun and there is a lot of empty space between the orbits.

The electrons don't orbit in nice flat elliptical planes, however. They whirl around in all kinds of 3D shapes from spheres to dumbbell shapes, and a myriad of others. These complex shaped orbits are called "electron shells." We can imagine it like the layers of an onion with many shells layered on top of each other. However, the shells don't touch or connect to each other. There is empty space between the shells where the electrons are forbidden to go by the laws of physics. The empty space is a type of energy barrier like the one we were discussing in the last section.

Each shell has an amount of energy associated with it. Inner shells have lower energy and outer shells have higher energy. The more energy an electron has, the bigger the orbit that it needs. It is similar to how a racecar that is going around a racetrack at high speed has to swing farther out than a car going slowly.

When a photon of light comes in and hits an electron orbiting an atom, it gets absorbed by the electron. As the photon is absorbed, it gives its energy to the electron. The electron now has too much energy for its energy level shell, so it quantum leaps out to the energy level shell that matches its new energy level. The higher energy level shell is called the "excited state," and the original shell where the electron usually lives is called the "ground state."

I previously mentioned that nothing in nature likes to be in a higher energy state and everything wants to go back to the ground state where it is less excited and more at rest. Electrons obey this law too. They don't want to be in the excited state and drop down to the ground state whenever they can.[1]

When the electron drops down to the ground state, it sends out a photon of light with the energy it needs to lose to match the energy shell that it is going to. This is the same amount of energy that the electron absorbed from the incoming photon in the first place. Therefore, it looks like the same photon comes out as the one that went in. To summarize the process: an electron absorbs a photon of light and jumps up to a higher energy level shell, then quickly emits an identical photon of light and drops back down to its original energy level shell. This is the quantum process responsible for every object reflecting light, which enables us to see everything that can be seen.

Now, here is the strange part: when the electron jumps up to a higher energy level shell or when it jumps back down, it does not physically go through the empty space between the shells. The empty space is a forbidden zone. The electrons are never allowed to be there and they never are. The electrons move from one orbit to another without ever physically existing in the middle! It is like jumping from Earth to Mars without going in between. This is called, "Quantum Leaping."

---

[1] The average time that it takes for an electron to drop back down to the ground state is called the half-life. Half of the time, the electron will drop down faster than the half-life and half of the time it will take longer. There needs to be a random quantum fluctuation to start the process of dropping back down, so there is a random distribution of drop down times around the mean. It is a similar concept and process to the half-life for radioactive decay.

Wave Function at Different Energy Levels

Total Wave Function with Interference

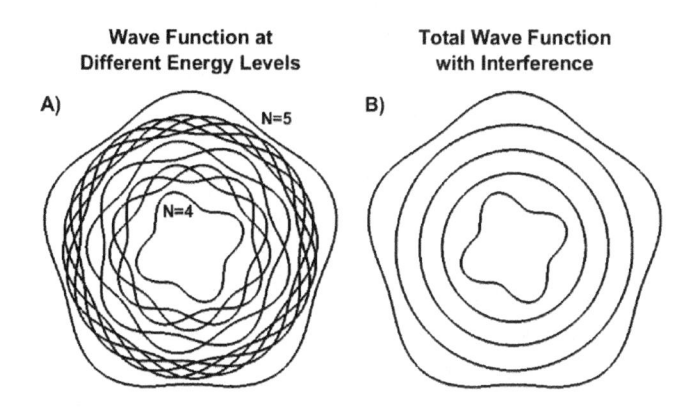

Figure 10: A simple sketch of an electron wave function in 2D. The real wave function is waving in many complex 3D shapes. A) The component wave showing interference at various radii. B) The total wavefunction that we can measure.

It sounds crazy and impossible, doesn't it? Here again, the wave nature of the electrons helps make this seemingly impossible phenomenon possible. Let's simplify things down to a 2D sketch to help us visualize the wave (see Figure 10). When a wave goes around in a circle, it must meet itself at the same spot when it gets all the way around. If it doesn't, it will destructively interfere with itself. In Figure 10-A, I have illustrated the wave pattern (called the wave function) at several different radii. At the innermost radius and the outermost radius, the wave function meets itself, but for the middle radii, the wave function doesn't meet itself. As the wave goes around, it overlaps and interferes with itself. The peaks and valleys overlap and perfectly cancel each other out all the way around the circle. Therefore, the total wave pattern is flat as shown in Figure 10-B.

I previously mentioned that we can only measure the total wave pattern of all the waves put together. This is true for physical and nonphysical waves. Therefore, if the total wave pattern is flat, we can't measure any waving there. If there is no waving, there is no physical manifestation of the quantum particle. When there is no physical manifestation of the particle, we say that it does not physically exist.

As the electron absorbs the energy from an incoming photon, it increases the radius of its orbit. Immediately, it begins to destructively interfere with itself causing it to pop out of physical existence. Once it gets to the energy level that matches its new energy level, the electron begins to constructively interfere with itself again. Then, the total wave pattern is observable again, which means the electron pops back into physical existence. The reverse process happens as the electron emits a photon to drop back down to the ground state.[2]

One important thing to note is that even though the electron disappears from human observation, the energy is still there and the underlying nonphysical waves are still waving and still moving to the target orbit. However, we have no way to measure the component waves. We can only measure the total pattern, which is temporarily zero.

---

[2] Another way to think about it is to employ the tunneling concept that we talked about in the last section. The electron tunnels through the energy barrier of the empty space and pops out on the other side. However, in this case, the event is driven by an increase or decrease in energy and happens every time. In the previous section, the energy level remained the same, so tunneling happens very rarely.

Teleportation

The concepts of quantum leaping and quantum tunneling sound a lot like the concept of teleportation, don't they? There are examples of many different theories about teleportation in sci-fi movies, TV, and novels, but the "science" in fiction isn't always the same as the science in reality. However, the Bible has many references to teleportation actually occurring.[3] It is not fiction.

> *Acts 8:39-40 NASB, "When they came up out of the water, the Spirit of the Lord snatched Philip away; and the eunuch no longer saw him, but went on his way rejoicing. But Philip found himself at Azotus, and as he passed through he kept preaching the gospel to all the cities until he came to Caesarea."*

Most of the references to the teleportation type events in the Bible use similar phrasing to each other, in essence saying something to the effect of "The Spirit lifted them up and took them away."

There are a few different ways to think about this concept. The first way is to lift the quantum particles that make up the person out of the physical dimensions and into the nonphysical/spiritual dimensions. To simplify things for illustration purposes, we can squish down 3D space-time into a line and just look at a particle on that line. Then, we can put the next nonphysical dimension perpendicular to the

---

[3] 1 Kings 18:12, 2 Kings 2:16, Ezekiel 3:14-15, John 6:21, John 20:19

A) **Higher Dimensional Teleportation**

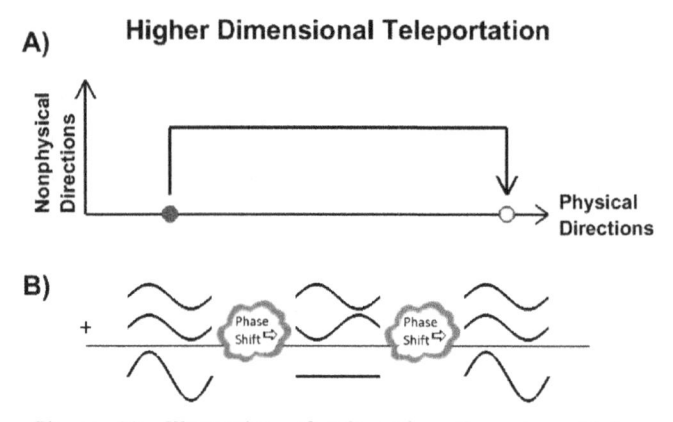

Figure 11: Illustration of teleporting through a higher dimension. A) A particle moves off the physical line into a higher nonphysical dimension and then back again. B) The particle's component quantum waves are phase shifted to cancel out the physical total wave pattern and then phase shifted back again.

line. This will help us imagine what is going on (see Figure 11-A).

When a quantum particle is lifted off of the physical line, the particle no longer exists in physical space-time. The quantum particle can then be moved to another location and put back so that it is on the physical line again. Once the quantum particle is back on the line, it now exists in physical space-time again. In this way, the quantum particles, and the person they make up, can move from one space-time location to another without physically going in between. This concept matches the phrasing in most of the Scripture references to teleportation-like phenomena, where the Spirit of God lifts the person up and takes them away so that they disappear from one place and appear in another.

Another way to think about it is to phase shift the quantum waves that make up the person so that the total quantum wave pattern is only vibrating in the nonphysical dimensions. Thus, the physical wave pattern will be flat just like in the quantum leaping discussion from the last section (see Figure 11-B). When the total wave pattern in the physical dimensions is flat, the person will not be physically present anywhere in physical space-time. The underlying waves and their energy can then be moved somewhere else. Then, the quantum waves can be phase shifted back so that the total wave pattern is vibrating in the physical dimensions again. Through phase shifting the component quantum waves, the person can disappear from one space-time location and reappear in another space-time location.

We can visualize it like an iceberg where the part that sticks out of the water is the physical part and everything under the water is the nonphysical/spiritual part. If we push the iceberg under water, it will be invisible in the physical realm. The iceberg can then be quickly moved and popped back up so that it can be seen again. From the point of view of someone stuck on the surface of the water with no knowledge of what happens under the water, it would look like the iceberg teleported from one place to another.

We can only comprehend the physical dimensions where someone is in one physical location and then is in another physical location without physically traveling in between. We call it teleportation because we can't see the movement that is happening in the nonphysical/spiritual dimensions.

Wormhole Teleportation

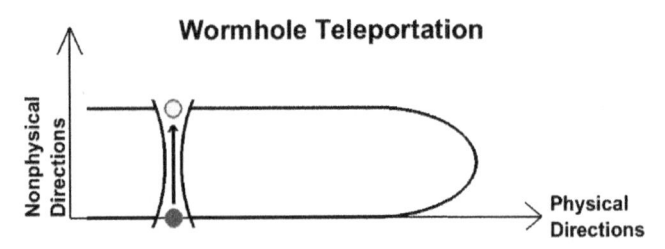

Figure 12: Illustration of a wormhole allowing a particle to jump from one space-time point to another without going in between.

Another way to think about it is the concept of a wormhole (see Figure 12). A wormhole is a shortcut through the higher dimensions. We can think of the physical dimensions as a flat piece of paper. If we bend the piece of paper through a higher dimension so that two distant points touch, we can jump from one point to another through the wormhole connecting the two distinct points without going in between.

All three of these ways of thinking about teleporting are actually the same thing. Although it might not be obvious at first glance, all three methods are essentially saying that the quantum particles (and thus the person) must become entirely spirit/nonphysical for a moment. We must allow every fiber of our being to slosh over into being entirely spiritual and completely let go of being physical. We can then move somewhere and allow every fiber of our being to slosh back into being both physical and spiritual, and then hope we end up with the same thing we started with!

This process is extraordinarily complex even for the smallest quantum particle. I may have made it sound simple in my naïve hand-wavy argument, but in reality, it is practically impossible without help from a higher dimensional being. Every single electron and quark in every single atom in every single cell in the whole body would have to move simultaneously and come back into the same configuration it left in the same position it was in relative to all the others. The amount of data needed to store the state is massive. We would also have to calculate how to uniquely phase shift each of the practically infinite number of quantum waves on both ends of the process to get the quantum waves to cancel each other out in the middle. Even with the amazing power of our modern day computers, I'm not sure we are capable of doing the necessary calculations in a reasonable amount of time or of storing the data.

Besides, we still can't even measure the component quantum waves or the nonphysical higher dimensions yet. We have no way, at present, to individually manipulate the component quantum waves in the necessary manner to achieve the desired effect in the total physical wave pattern. Even if we could do the theoretical calculations, we have no way to actually accomplish phase shifting the quantum waves to move them into another dimension. Therefore, there is no way, at present, for human beings to teleport even a single quantum particle using these methods.

Miracles

God, however, is sustaining the whole universe in the quantum fields and has full access to the component quantum waves. He is certainly smart enough and in control enough to easily manipulate the quantum wave patterns to change the manifestation in the physical to anything He wants. God can manipulate the quantum wave patterns to make anything happen at every level, whether small or big.

Using the concept of quantum leaping and teleporting through higher dimensions, we can see one possible way that God can do many of the miracles we see recorded in the Bible and have heard testimonies about in our modern world. Growing out arms, dissolving tumors, multiplying food, healing sickness, changing water into wine[4], and many other miracles are all easy when one has full access to teleporting particles around in very precise ways.

God does not have to break any laws of physics to do His miracles. He can just use the laws He made in a very clever manner. We don't know if God uses the concept of teleporting particles to do these types of miracles or if He uses some other phenomenon that we haven't discovered yet. What we do know is that it is possible within the laws of nature for these types of miracles to occur, if the One doing the miracles is extremely smart, massively powerful, and completely understands the laws of nature. Humans are not any of those things, so we can't perform these types of miracles. However, just because we can't do something, doesn't mean that God can't do something.

---

[4] There are too many verses to list all of miracles and healings in Scripture, but here are a few: 1 Kings 13:4-6, Matthew 8:16, 12:10-15, Matthew 15:34-38, Luke 9:12-17, John 2:3-11, Acts 3:2-8, 5:16

Chapter 5
Quantum Unity

Most people are familiar with the three phases of matter that we learn about in elementary school: solids, liquids, and gases. Each phase of matter deals with the same material, but that material behaves very differently in each phase. Ice, water, and steam are all H_2O, but they all have different properties and behaviors from each other. In scientific terms, different scientific laws dominate the properties and behavior of a substance in each phase, but the substance itself remains the same.

There are also two more phases of matter besides solids, liquids, and gases. They are the plasma phase and the condensed phase. Typically, as the temperature increases, a substance will change from the solid phase to the liquid phase then to the gas phase. When a substance gets extremely hot, like in the Sun and in fusion experiments, it will enter the plasma phase. On the other end of the spectrum, when certain substances get extremely cold, they enter the condensed phase. However, the condensed phase can occur in solid, liquid, and gas form, so it is a very unique phase of matter. We don't experience these extreme temperatures in normal life, so we aren't familiar with them.

We tend to call the condensed phase "super." When it occurs in a solid, it is called a superconductor. When it occurs in a liquid, it is called a superfluid. However, when it occurs in a gas, it is just called a condensate, or more formally, a Bose-Einstein Condensate (BEC). It is named after the scientists who first worked out the mathematical theory that predicted how condensates work in gases.

Quantum Physics Made Visible

The condensed phase of matter is a quantum physical effect. All the quantum physical laws that dominate the behavior of the tiniest quantum particles in the universe also apply to the condensed phase of matter. However, a condensate can be large enough to see with the naked eye. We can see and hold superconductors and experience the strangeness of the quantum realm in everyday life. We can also see superfluids, but they are much too cold to touch. This quantum phase of matter allows us to see the quantum behavior of things that are normally too small to see. Thus, a condensate allows us to see all the weird quantum physical phenomena with our own eyes.

Each phase of matter has very different properties and behavior than all the others. We are used to the difference between solids, liquids, and gases, but the properties and behavior of condensed matter are very different from anything we are used to.

For example, a superconductor will easily float on top of a magnet without losing stability and falling off. A normal magnet with the correct polarity will float for a moment, but then it will be pulled to one side or another and fall off or get attached to the lower magnet. A superconductor, however, is content to float above a magnet forever. The superconductor must be kept very cold, at about 72 Kelvin (-201 °C) or less depending on the type of material it is made out of. If the superconductor doesn't warm up and turn back into a normal solid, it will float over the magnet forever. This happens because superconductor repels the magnetic field, which allows them to float.

Superconductors also have no electrical resistance. That means that they don't heat up or lose energy when a current flows through it like normal conductors do. Your laptop gets hot because of the heat generated by the current flowing through all the circuits. If the circuits were made out of superconductors, however, it would never heat up. A current flowing through a superconductor will continue to flow forever, since there is no energy loss. The electrons in a superconducting wire can move past every obstacle with no resistance. There is nothing that can hinder their flow.

Another example is superfluid Helium, which is still a liquid, but it behaves very differently than normal liquids. Liquid Helium must be cooled down to below approximately 2 Kelvin (-271 °C) in order to enter into the condensed phase. That's an extremely cold 2 degrees above absolute zero! Needless to say, it's pretty hard to get the liquid that cold, and we can only do it in the laboratory. There are lots of cool videos on the internet demonstrating the strange things that superfluid Helium and other superfluids can do. You can also just search for superfluid videos on the internet and find lots of them.

As the liquid Helium is cooling down to the transition point, it boils and churns as the warmer atoms evaporate away. Immediately after the transition, the superfluid suddenly becomes completely still. Becoming a superfluid immediately put all the atoms into the rest state when they were all moving around chaotically just a moment before.

A superfluid also has many other odd characteristics. It has no viscosity, which is like friction for liquids. That means that it doesn't stick to anything, not even the walls of the container. Because, it doesn't stick to anything, it doesn't lose energy when it spins or flows in a current. Therefore, a current in the superfluid will flow forever, and a vortex will spin forever.

The superfluid can climb the steepest walls because it has infinite surface tension. It can also flow through the smallest crack, which makes it very hard to keep inside its container. All of these zeros and infinities make condensed matter have very interesting properties indeed.

Quantum Spin

In order to understand this unique phase of matter, we first need to understand "spin." Every quantum particle has a characteristic that we call "spin." Even though the quantum particles are not physically spinning like a top, they act as if they are, so we call that characteristic "spin." Remember that quantum particles are only marginally physical, so they can't really do anything physically. However, quantum particles follow the same rules that spinning tops do, so we say they have spin.

Everything in quantum physics is quantized which is where the name comes from. "Quantized" means that only certain values are allowed and they have to be evenly spread out. Quantum spin is also quantized. The constant spacing between the values is 1/2, which means that we can only have whole integer and half-integer spin values.

This leads to two categories of particles. The ones with integer spin (0, 1, 2 ...) are called Bosons. The particles with half-integer spin (1/2, 3/2, 5/2 ...) are called Fermions. Photons, which are particles of light, are Bosons. Some atoms are also Bosons. Electrons and some other atoms are Fermions. There are no values for spin other than half-integer and integer values, but the spin can be positive or negative. The sign on the spin tells us which way the particle would be spinning if it were physically spinning like a top, clockwise or counter-clockwise.

These two categories of particles have very different properties and behavior. The most important one for this discussion is called the "Pauli Exclusion Principle." It states that Bosons are very "social" and love to be in the same state as other Bosons. Fermions, however, are very "anti-social" and will never be in exactly the same state as another identical Fermion. For example, photons of light will bunch

Bosons **Fermions**

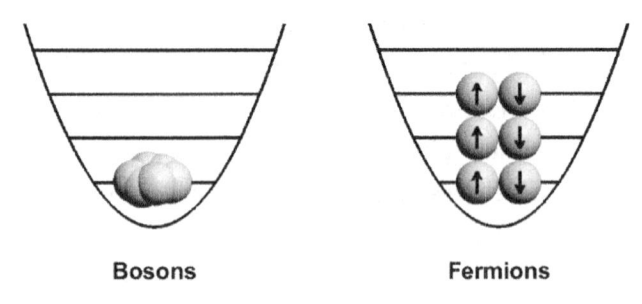

Figure 13: Bosons are "social" an all occupy the same lowest energy state. Fermions are "anti-social" and all occupy distinct energy states.

together into the same lowest energy state, but we will never find electrons in exactly the same state as each other (see Figure 13). Once one energy state is occupied by one positive spin electron and one negative spin electron pair, the next electron has to go to the next higher energy state. This fact is very fundamental to the entire field of chemistry, but I won't get into the details of chemistry here.

Bose-Einstein Condensation only happens with Bosons, as the name implies. The social behavior of Bosons allows the atoms or molecules to condense into the same lowest energy state. The same process works with superconductors and superfluids as it does for Bose-Einstein Condensates. However, a super conductor works with electron pairs. The Fermionic electrons pair up to form a unit so that the half-integer spins add up to an integer value of 0 or 1. Then, the pair of electrons as a unit act like a Boson, which can then condense into a super conducting state. Superfluids and BECs work with Bosons directly.

Heisenberg Uncertainty Principle

In chapter 1, we discussed how all quantum particles are really made up of many quantum waves interfering with each other to make a relatively localized wave packet. The wave packets have tails that spread out everywhere, but are so small that they have a negligible effect on anything around them.

We also talked about how asking the questions of where the wave packet is and how fast it is going are very difficult questions to answer. Pure waves are spread out and don't have a precise location, but they do have a precise frequency. Particles, on the other hand, have a precise location, but do not have a precise frequency. The frequency of the waves directly turns into momentum in the quantum world. Wave packets are somewhere in the middle of the spectrum with a vague position and a vague momentum/frequency.

For quantum particles, which are really wave packets, there is a distribution of momenta in all the component quantum waves and the packet has a width to it. Therefore, we can't measure only one momentum or position for any quantum particle. This is called the Heisenberg uncertainty principle. The principle states that we can't measure the exact position and exact momentum of a quantum particle at the same time, and that the more precisely we measure the position, the less precisely we can measure the momentum, and vice versa.

That means that the more we try to squeeze the particle into an exact position to make the wave packet more like a single pulse, the more component waves we need to put into the wave packet. That, in turn, results in a much broader distribution of momenta. If we want to measure the momentum (essentially the frequency) of the particle, we need it to be more wave-like so that it has a single momentum. In order to do that, we have to spread out the wave packet, which obviously makes it harder to nail down exactly where it is. Our ability to measure both position and momentum simultaneously is uncertain.

Since we can't measure the nonphysical component quantum waves with our current technology, we are forced to squeeze the particles down to be able to measure them in the physical realm. This causes us to lose a lot of information about them. However, the Heisenberg uncertainty principle is not just due to the limitations of our experimental equipment. It is more fundamental than that. It is actually inherent in the nature of the wave packets themselves because of how they are made out of the component quantum waves.

When we develop experimental equipment that can measure a distribution of momenta simultaneously or measure a spread out position or can measure the underlying quantum waves themselves, then we will know a lot more about what is going on under the hood with the quantum particles. The uncertainty principle, however, will still be operating in full force. If we squeeze the particle down in one direction or another, it will get bigger in the other direction. There is no way around that.

Cooling Quantum Particles

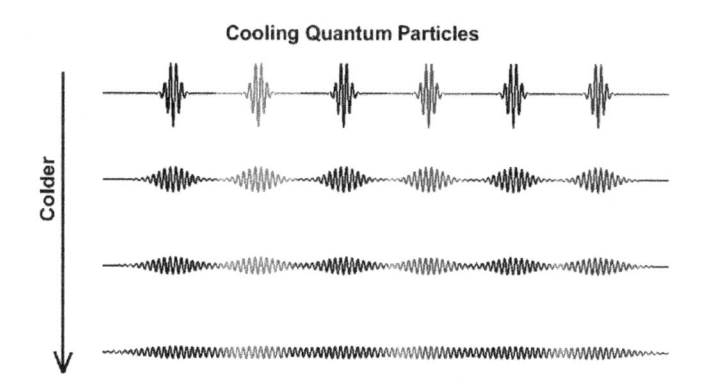

Colder ↓

Figure 14: The wave packets spread out as the temperature decreases. When the temperature gets cold enough, the tails overlap enough to cause the wave functions to synchronize.

Making a Condensate

In order to make a Bose-Einstein Condensate, superfluid, or superconductor, we have to get the Bosonic atoms or electron pairs very, very cold. The colder the atoms get, the slower they move, which means smaller momentum. The uncertainty principle tells us that as the momentum gets smaller, the position (width) of the wave packet gets wider. Then, the tiny little tails that were barely overlapping before start getting bigger and bigger (see Figure 14). That causes the interaction between neighboring particles to become stronger and stronger. When there is enough overlap between the tails of the wave packets, they synchronize with each other.

Because the bosons are social and everything likes to be in the lowest energy state possible, as soon as they sync up, they exchange information about the lowest state that any of them are occupying, then they all immediately condense into that lowest energy state. When the bosons were separated, they couldn't find the path to get to the lower energy state, so they couldn't go there. They need each other's help to all move into the ground state together where they can be at rest as much as possible.

Quantum Unity

In the condensed state, all the atoms are operating in perfect unity. They are all doing the same thing at the same time and are all in the same state. There is also so much overlap between them that no one can tell where one ends and the next one begins. The atoms are like one big object doing one thing rather than a bunch of individual objects each doing their own separate thing.

When the atoms, molecules, or electron pairs are in this completely unified state, the bulk material has all the "super" properties that I described before. It is the unity among the quantum particles that gives rise to no resistance, no energy loss, currents that last forever, superfluids climbing up walls and flowing through the smallest crack, and superconductors floating on the magnetic field.

All the individual parts are acting as one big unified object without counteracting each other. That unity aligns and magnifies the quantum phenomena and makes it visible to us. Thus, they have all these "super powers," which are really just normal quantum abilities.

God's eternal purpose is for all things to be united in Christ both on earth and in heaven:

Ephesians 1:9-10 ESV, "making known to us the mystery of his will, according to his purpose, which he set forth in Christ as a plan for the fullness of time, to unite all things in him, things in heaven and things on earth."

What would it be like if the Body of Christ actually entered into a completely unified state where each individual member was completely unified with all the others and with the Head, Jesus Christ? What would happen if our spirits were unified with all of our brothers and sisters' spirits and with God's Spirit? All of our innate spiritual abilities would be aligned and magnified for the entire world to see.

However, getting to that unified state is not easy. As we cool the atoms down, the harder it gets to cool them down further. The closer we get to the transition point, the exponentially harder it gets. We have to put in a great deal of effort to get a little bit of progress. Then, we put in even more effort and get even less progress. It can be very discouraging.

This seems very much like life sometimes. However, the curves do cross at some point. It does not take an infinite amount of effort to get to the transition point. It is very hard, but it is not impossible. We must not give up, we must keep going, and we must not let ourselves get discouraged by the small amount of progress. The circumstances are very difficult because we are so close to our breakthrough. The difficulty is evidence that the transition point is very close. We have to maintain our perspective on what is really happening and not get distracted by the difficulties in our temporary circumstances.

On the other side of the transition, things suddenly get significantly better. Besides all of the other "super" properties of being in a condensate, we can now put in a little effort and see incredible progress. Every little bit of effort that we put in is multiplied by being unified with everyone else and great progress is made by all.

Let's keep our eyes on Jesus and what He is doing rather than on our difficult circumstances. God is working to bring us into complete unity with Him and with each other. Let's cooperate with Him and surrender to the process, no matter how difficult and challenging it is to come into unity with those around us. God has a way through the Cross of Jesus to take care of all our wanting to do things our own way (sin and rebellion) and help us do things in the most restful productive way (His way). All we have to do is accept His brilliant ways rather than trusting in our own limited perspective. We need to allow ourselves to rest in Him and let God work through us.

Chapter 6
Quantum Observation

One of the most fundamental and most misunderstood experiments in all of quantum physics is the "double slit experiment." It is said that if you can understand the double-slit experiment, you can understand all of quantum physics. It is abundantly clear from all of the supposed "explanations" out there, however, that very few people actually understand the experiment or its implications about the nature of the universe.

The double-slit experiment explicitly shows the fundamental wave-particle nature inherent in quantum particles as we discussed in Chapter 1. The experiment also clearly displays the limitations our 4D physical equipment has when measuring higher dimensional nonphysical quantum particles. Of special note, the experiment shows the strong interaction between our ability to observe and measure the quantum particles and the behavior of the quantum particles themselves. On first blush, it appears that our ability to observe the quantum particles somehow completely changes their behavior, and when we are not looking, they behave differently.

This is another example of how the quantum nature of the universe is totally contrary to our everyday experience. Physical objects behave the same way when we are looking at them as they do when we are not looking at them. Just like the other quantum phenomena we have discussed, the results of the double slit experiment seem counter-intuitive and even out right impossible in classical mechanics.

Many have tried to explain the results of the double slit experiment in terms of everyday 4D concepts (like time and physical objects) and have come up with all kinds of complicated and crazy sounding theories. Many of these theories have ended up in popular fiction and non-fiction, because they sound "cool" and fascinating. Many people may even believe that these highly popularized explanations are what science says is correct. This is not the case. Just because you may have read something in ten books or seen a documentary on it, doesn't make it true. In this chapter, I will try to set the record straight.

Quantum effects can't be explained with classical concepts. Quantum physics is fundamentally different. Any theory that tries to explain these nonphysical quantum effects in a limited 4D physical box will utterly fail to accurately describe and predict the physics. Nonphysical objects don't follow physical rules, and we shouldn't expect them to. However, that doesn't mean that all the confusion

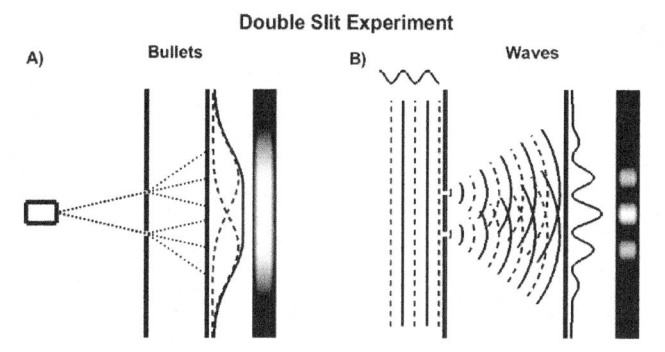

Figure 15: Double Slit experimental setup. A) The experiment performed with bullets. The total number (solid line) is the sum of the distributions from each slit separately (dashed lines). B) The experiment performed with water waves. The intensity shows interference from the wave diffracted from the two slits.

surrounding the double slit experiment can't be cleared up with a proper understanding of the true wave packet nature of the quantum particles.

Classical Double Slit Experiment

First, let's describe the actual experiment and then we can discuss the interpretation of the results. The experiment takes quantum particles, like electrons or photons, and fires them one at a time at a wall with two narrow slits in it, which are very close together. Behind the slits is another wall with a detector screen to tell us where the quantum particles hit the wall. Let's look at what happens in our everyday world first, and then compare that to what happens in the quantum world.

When we do the experiment with particles like bullets being fired at a target (see Figure 15-A), they hit the first wall somewhere and are not counted, or they go through exactly one of the slits, hit the detector screen, and are then counted. We can think of the detector screen in this example like the piece of target paper that shows where the bullets hit in target practice. We change out the target paper frequently so we can tell if a bullet hits in the same spot more than once. We will also fire the gun slowly so only one bullet hits the detector screen at a time.

After the experiment, we count how many bullets hit in each spot on the detector screen. Then, we plot the results, which are shown by the solid line on the right hand side of the detector screen in Figure 15-A. As we would expect, we see two groups of bullet holes in the detector screen right behind the slits. Some of the bullets have ricocheted off the edges of the slits and spread out from the center of the slit. The two slits are very close together, so the spread from the bullets hitting the sides overlaps with the other slit. We therefore see one big group of bullet holes in the center and less and less bullet holes as we get farther from the center.

If we add up the bullets that came through the top slit with the ones that came through the bottom slit (dashed lines in figure 15-A), we will get the total number of bullets that came through (the solid line). We can verify this by closing one of the slits and repeating the experiment. Then, we repeat with the other slit open and the first one closed. Bullets are things we are familiar with, and they behave in a way we expect.

On the other hand, if we do the experiment with water waves, we get different results because of the wave nature of the water. The intensity of the wave that hits the detector screen is plotted on the right hand side of the screen in Figure 15-B. When the water waves hit the two slits, they "diffract" out in circles, because the water drags on the edges of the slits and slows it down a little relative to the center part. This is similar to the ricochet situation with the bullets, but fluid dynamics is causing the effect rather than molecules bouncing off the walls. This causes the waves to spread out rather than hitting the detector screen straight on, in the same manner that the bullets were spread out from hitting the edges.

Since the water waves are waves, the two sets of ripples will interfere with each other. That means the amplitude of the waves from the top and bottom slits add up. Where there are two peaks, the total will be higher. Where there are two valleys, the total will be lower. Where a peak and a valley overlap they will cancel each other out and the total will be flatter. For the bullets, we added up the number of bullets that hit in each spot on the detector. For water waves, we add up the amplitude of the waves at each spot on the detector.

Because of the interference of the waves, the total pattern that we see on the detector screen will be a series of peaks and valleys, which become smaller as they go farther from the center. The waves are traveling out in circles and the screen is flat. As we go farther away from the slits, the water will be less and less disturbed by the waves from the slits, so we don't see an effect.

For waves, we look at the total wave pattern of the energy that is traveling from the source to the screen, not the individual particles that make up the water (the "medium") that the wave is traveling in. The unseen energy wave is what experiences the interference and moves the water molecules around, but we can only see the physical result of where there are more and less water molecules. We then have to infer what is happening with the underlying energy wave.

There are some similarities and some differences in the particle case and the wave case. In both cases, the particles and the waves spread out from the slits, and then we add up whatever we are measuring at each unique position on the detector screen for a specific amount of time. We have to add up the results from a large number of particles (bullets or water molecules) to see the pattern in both cases. We also add up what we are measuring from each individual slit to get the total measurement for both cases.

However, what we measure in each case is different. For particles, we measure the number of particles at each location. For waves, we measure the intensity (energy rate) of the wave at each location, which we derive from the amplitude of the wave. Also, we have to be careful to add the amplitudes from each slit first and then derive the intensity. We can't add the two intensities from each slit and get the total intensity, because the order of the operators changes the results.

Quantum Double Slit Experiment

Now, let's look at what happens with electrons or any other quantum particles. For electrons, we use an electron gun, which fires electrons at the two slits one at a time. We then measure where each electron hits on the detector screen. After a large number of electrons hit the screen, we plot the results and compare it to what we expect.

If the electrons were particles, like little bullets, we would measure the same pattern as the bullets since we are counting the number of the electrons, not the energy of the electrons, but we don't. We measure the wavy interference pattern, just like water waves! We aren't measuring the intensity of a wave in a sea of electrons. We are measuring the number of discrete electrons sent in one at a time.[1] The electrons leave the electron gun as discrete entities one at a time and arrive at the detector screen in one spot as discrete entities. However, the pattern of where the electrons hit the screen is that of a wave that has interfered with itself. That sounds strange doesn't it?

To get an interference pattern, we have to add up the amplitudes of some waves that are diffracted from both slits. For the water waves, there was a very large number of molecules bouncing around under the influence of the energy wave and colliding with each other. However, for the electron scenario, there is only one electron traveling through the system at a time. Being quantum particles, the electrons are quantized. That means that they can't break in

---

[1] The fundamentalist quantum physicist might well argue that measuring the intensity of a wave in the "electron sea" is the same thing as measuring the number of electrons, just as measuring the varying number of water molecules at the screen will give us the information to obtain the intensity of the water wave. However, the details of that argument are well beyond the scope of this book.

half with each half going through one slit and then interfering with itself. The electrons must remain whole. Thus, the particles can't be colliding with themselves to cause the interference pattern, so how can it be interfering with itself?

Quantum Waves Again

People want the electrons to go through all kinds of complicated gymnastics to try to explain the results, but it's not that hard. The quantum wave packet once again comes to the rescue and makes everything remarkably simple and straightforward. Remember the unseen energy wave was what caused the interference in the water waves, not the collisions of the molecules themselves. The collisions were a secondary effect. We shouldn't expect collisions of the particles or anything so physical to be the cause here, either.

As we have discussed several times now, the electron, like all quantum particles, is a wave packet. That means that the localized total wave pattern is made up of a large number of component waves that are spread out with varying frequencies and amplitudes (see Figure 16). We can't measure or observe the component waves, only the total wave packet, and even then, we can only really measure one point at a time. When there is a higher magnitude in the total wave pattern, we measure that point more often than when there is a lower magnitude. We can only measure points, but the quantum particle is really a wave packet made up of lots of spread out quantum waves.

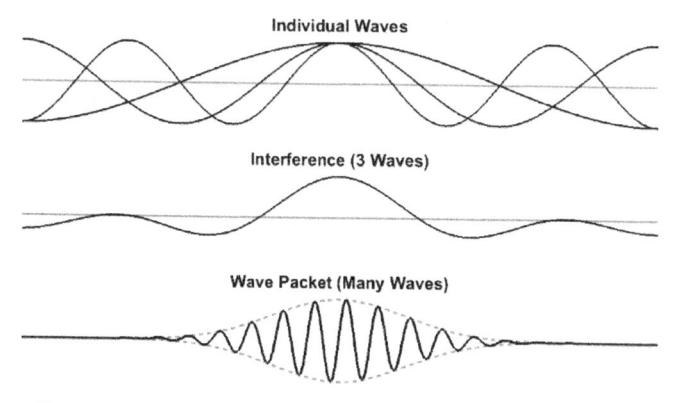

Figure 16: Wave interference adds up to make a wave packet.

A localized particle would travel in a straight line, go through one of the slits, and then go on to hit the detector screen. On the other hand, the underlying component waves are waves. The underlying quantum waves hit both slits and diffract out in circles that interfere just like the water waves. When the underlying waves change, so does the total wave pattern. When the total wave pattern changes, so does what we measure. The single points that we measure as the electrons are entirely determined by the total wave pattern. It's very straightforward.

This is how one electron can interfere with itself without "breaking in half." Waves don't break in half; they bend around things. However, we can only measure one point on the total wave packet at a time, so our measurements show a quantized whole electron at all times.

When both slits are open, the electrons hit the screen in an interference pattern because, under the hood, they are made out of waves. We are simply adding up the amplitudes of the component quantum waves from both slits and getting a new total wave pattern for the electron. It's pretty simple, really. The fact that we see an interference pattern proves that the electrons are made out of underlying quantum waves.

If we close one of the slits, there is no second diffraction pattern of quantum ripples to interfere with, so we expect to see the same distribution pattern as for particles and waves. It is difficult to tell the difference between the pattern for particles and waves from just one slit. That same single slit pattern is what we see in the experiment too, which makes sense.

However, when we look at the number of electrons that come through each slit in each location on the screen, it doesn't add up to the interference pattern on the screen, so some people get confused. If there is no opportunity for the quantum ripples in the component waves to interfere, it will give a different pattern than when there is an opportunity to interfere. I'll explain more about that in the next section. Just remember for now that the electron is a wave packet whose component waves are interfering with themselves, but we can only measure point particles.

Which Slit?

The next question people naturally ask to try to understand the quantum two slit experiment further is, "which slit did the electron go through on its way to the screen?" This is a nonsensical question, but that never stopped anyone. The question makes sense in the physical world, but it doesn't make sense in the quantum world.

When we do the experiments to try to determine which slit the electron goes through, it destroys the interference pattern and the electrons behave just like the bullets, so we see particle-like behavior. On the other hand, if we don't look at which slit the electrons are going through, the interference pattern is restored, so we see wave-like behavior. Therefore, it seems on the surface that our knowing about "which slit" somehow changes the behavior of the electrons. This is contrary to the way things work in the visible world, and is therefore quite confusing.

The electron isn't really a physical object that should be constrained to follow 3D physical rules like going through a path only one way or another. Bullets would only go through one slit because they are physical objects. However, electrons are not like bullets, and they are not like simple water waves. They are more like a hybrid of both, because they are a wave packet of nonphysical quantum waves. Quantum particles have some characteristics of particles and some characteristics of simple waves, and they have other characteristics that aren't either one.

However, in the early days of quantum mechanics, the nonphysical nature of the wave packet wasn't very well understood. It is natural for everyone to keep thinking in terms of physical objects that we all understand, and then compare and contrast that with the data for the quantum particles. Unfortunately, that comparison quickly fell apart because quantum particles don't behave anything like the physical objects that we are used to. Still, people tried to make sense out of all the data using physical ideas. But, nonsensical questions lead to nonsensical answers. Trying to make sense out of that is just an exercise in futility.

The real problem here is that "which slit" is asking a physical particle question about a nonphysical quantum wave packet. All of our measurements can only measure particles at specific points, so it is easy to get confused and assume that particle type questions are reasonable things to ask about when we are not making a measurement. But, they're not.

One of the weirdest things in quantum physics is that quantum particles behave differently when they are being measured than when they aren't being observed. Therefore, we can't apply the same expectations to what is happening when we aren't looking as when we are. We shouldn't expect particle-like behavior in the middle of an experiment where we can't measure the quantum particles. We can only expect particle-like behavior at the source and the detectors.

Quantum Observation

We need to get some more clarity on what is happening differently when we are looking at the quantum particles than when we are not looking at them. The main thing we need to notice here is that "observing" the electrons is a very active and invasive process. We are not just glancing at the slits and passively observing which slit the electron goes through, as some explanations would lead you to believe. Observing any system requires disturbing the system in some way to get information about it out so we can see it.

When we look at a macroscopic object, like a book, the disturbance is so small that we never really notice. When we see the book, we are really recording a large number of photons coming from the book into our eyes. Every one of those photons came from some electron on the outside of the book quantum leaping down to its ground state and emitting a photon. Those electrons had already absorbed a photon from a light bulb or the sun to quantum leap up to the excited state to get the process started in the first place.

This change in state up and down to reflect the light into our eyes disturbs the electrons and changes their state. The electrons end up in the same state in which they started, so there is no net change there. However, the incoming photon gives a tiny little kick to the book and pushes on it ever so slightly. That kick is so small compared to the relatively giant book that we can barely measure the effect. Because of this, we say that in the visible world, we can measure and observe things without changing their state. Although, technically, the change was just too small to measure, so we ignored it.

In the quantum world, the photon and the electron are similar in "size," so the kickback from an incoming photon will make a sizable effect on the electron and change the direction it is moving in significantly. There are several other ways in quantum mechanics to observe what is happening with the electrons, but they too cause significant disturbances to the electron's motion. We currently have no way to get information about the electron without changing something about the electron. There is no such thing as passive observation.[2]

Quantum observation is violent, destructive, and very invasive. The quantum world is not visible. We have to change the quantum particles to make them visible, so we can tell what is going on with them. We aren't just glancing at the system and causing the outcome to change in some mysterious way. We are actively probing, squeezing, and altering the system, and then the system changes. When we change the system to observe it, it changes. This shouldn't be surprising.

When we look to see if the electrons are acting like particles at the slits, there is a different setup in the experiment than when we look to see if they are acting like waves. The change in the "maze" that the electrons are traversing causes them to take different paths. When we ask a particle question, we get a particle answer, and when we ask a wave question, we get a wave answer. It is very straightforward.

There is no need for mystical ways to explain how the electrons somehow knew ahead of time how we were going to look at them, and then seemingly changed their behavior according to the observer's thoughts, as some explanations claim. Many of the explanations I have read, heard, and seen sound like magicians doing sleight of hand; they want you to

---

[2] There is an entire field of quantum physics devoted to finding ways to do "non-destructive measurements." There has been some progress toward finding ways to measure a few systems without causing permanent damage to the state of the system, but there is still a long way to go.

look at what they want you to see and not look at what they are really doing. Many other explanations only mention specific aspects of the results and want the audience to completely ignore what is going on in all the other parts of the experiment. They make the obvious parts seem like magic and try to sell the audience on all kinds of mystical "realities" because they hide what is really happening. I hope to expose the magic trick and show everyone what is really happening so no one falls for what some others are trying to sell.

The electrons changed their behavior because we changed the maze through which we were sending them. They don't know about our thoughts and choices, but they do know about the lasers, electromagnetic fields, polarizing filters, lenses, walls, detectors and whatnot that we have put in their path. When we observe the electrons to tell which path they go through, we actively change them. Then, we get a different pattern on the detector screen. That makes sense. There is nothing mystical about it.

Quantum Eraser Experiment

You may be wondering if there is some other way to know which path the electrons took without changing them directly. The other way to know which path the electrons took through the slits is to separate the electron beams coming from the slits to make them go in different directions. Then, we can detect them on separate screens. This is the same as having one or the other slit closed. We just see two separate distribution patterns. The underlying

Simple Quantum Eraser

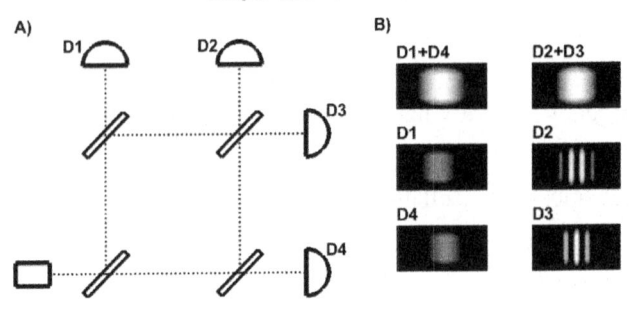

Figure 17: A) The setup for a simple quantum eraser experiment using 4 beam splitters. B) Simulated results for each detector.

quantum waves in the electrons have no chance to interact with the waves from the other slit, so there is no opportunity for interference to occur, so it doesn't. We just see single slit behavior. The same thing would happen with water waves.

If we bring the two electron beam paths back together and point them to the same spot, they have the chance to interfere with themselves again and they do. But, now we don't know which way they went through the slits either. Thus, we have effectively "erased" the which-path information and restored the interference pattern. When we knew which path the electrons took, there was no opportunity for them to interfere with themselves either. When we "erased" the which-path information, they had the opportunity to interfere, and they always do.

There are more complicated versions of the experiment that "erase" the which-path information after the experiment is over. In this case, we switch over to a photon beam coming from a laser to make things easier, but we are still sending photons through the slits one at a time. The photon beam is split twice, using beam splitters, producing four possible beam paths. One beam path from each slit is brought together and one is kept separate (see Figure 17). From looking at the results from all four detectors, we can see which slit the photon went through, and whether or not it interfered.

The experiment is conducted and all the photons are recorded hitting one of the four detectors in a specific location. Then, we choose to look only at the which-path information that we pull out of the beams that are separated. As expected, we see two distribution patterns that add up to one total distribution pattern, just as we saw with the bullets. Then, we decide to "erase" the which-path information and only look at the data from the beams that were brought together. As expected, we see an interference pattern. In this way, we are able to switch back and forth from seeing particle behavior to wave behavior in the photons based upon our choices well after the experiment is over.

Clearly, we could just as easily plot all the data from all four detectors at the same time and see both particle behavior and wave behavior at the same time, so we haven't really "erased" anything or made any "choices" that changed the behavior of the quantum particles. We have just chosen to look at one subset of the data or the other subset of the data, but both particle-like behavior and wave-like behavior are present in the data at all times, because the quantum particles are wave packets.

The quantum eraser phenomenon is just demonstrating how we can post-process the data to filter out one physical aspect or another from nonphysical higher dimensional objects. The quantum particles are really wave packets and not point particles or pure waves. The quantum particles have properties of particles and waves, but aren't purely either one.

When we filter out the data appropriately, we can see the particle properties of the localized wave packet, or we can see the spread out underlying wave properties that make up the wave packet. We aren't going back in time to change something that already happened and forcing the quantum particle to choose between being a particle or a wave. We are only choosing to look at one part of the data or the other, and then seeing a different side of a multifaceted object. However, the results are still very interesting as they point to the fact that the fullness of the quantum particles is much more that the physical particle or wave behavior that we can measure, and the results clearly demonstrate that the quantum particles are in fact wave packets.

Observation Changes Things

What we discover from the double slit experiment is that the quantum particles have both particle-like behavior and wave-like behavior and can display both at the same time. The experiment also clearly shows the wave packet properties of the quantum particles. No other mechanism is needed to fully explain the particle-like and wave-like behavior seen in the experiments.

From these experiments, we also discover that our observations do in fact change the outcome of the experiment, but not is some strange mystical way. We are actively interfering with the quantum particles and changing something about them in order to measure them, or we are filtering the data after the fact and only looking at certain facets of the quantum particle's behavior.

Some explanations of the double slit experiment require some kind of consciousness in the electrons or photons to know what the observer is thinking and to respond appropriately. This is completely unnecessary. The quantum particles are simply acting like the nonphysical higher dimensional wave packets that they are. We have to squeeze the quantum particles down into something remotely physical in order to observe them, which changes them. There is nothing more complicated, strange, or mystical than this going on.

How we choose to measure the quantum particles limits the measurement outcomes that we can record. We need to be careful not to confuse our limited measurements with the full reality of the quantum particles. How we choose to view the quantum realm changes how we perceive the quantum realm, but it doesn't change the reality of the quantum realm itself. How we choose to observe quantum objects limits the options and filters the data, so our perception is limited. However, our perception of reality isn't reality itself!

This principle works in our everyday lives, too. How we choose to look at the world around us strongly affects how we perceive the world around us. If we think that everything is horrible, we will filter out all the good that happens and only focus on the all the bad that happens. If we believe that everything is great, we will see all the good that happens and ignore all the bad that happens. However, in reality, some good things are happening and some bad things are happening. We instinctively filter the data that we perceive so that only information that supports our beliefs gets through and all the other information gets ignored. This reinforces our preconceived belief system so that it becomes stronger and stronger. This is simply human nature.

> *1 Corinthians 13:9-12, "For we know in part and we prophesy in part, but when completeness comes, what is in part disappears. When I was a child, I talked like a child, I thought like a child, I reasoned like a child. When I became a man, I put the ways of childhood behind me. For now we see only a reflection as in a mirror; then we shall see face to face. Now I know in part; then I shall know fully, even as I am fully known."*

All of us are inherently limited in our ability to perceive and understand the fullness of reality. We need humility to remember that the way we perceive the world around us is not necessarily the fullness of what is actually going on. Only God knows what is really real and what is actually going on. As we keep in close connection with Him and develop deeper communication with the Holy Spirit, He will teach us and continue to reveal the truth to us. The more we see God and know God, the more the fullness comes. God will show us where our preconceived beliefs are not lining up with reality and help us adjust our thinking to line up with reality. God will help us to perceive the world and the people around us more truthfully, if we ask Him to.

Chapter 7
Q & A

If all matter is made up of spiritual waves, does everything have a spirit?

Science is only just beginning to understand about the spiritual substance that makes up all the matter and light in the universe. Science hasn't discovered anything about sentient spirit beings of any kind at this point. However, the Bible says that the Holy Spirit, human spirits, and other spirit beings such as angels and demons exist in our universe. The Bible clearly differentiates between these different types of spiritual entities, although other religions don't have such distinctions. Let's look at some of the differences and similarities to help us get a better understanding.

All throughout the Scriptures, the Bible talks about how God created and gave life to every living thing. But, what is the actual difference between things that are alive and things that are not? Philosophers and scientists have been arguing for millennia about what makes a person or even an animal a "living being" without ever being able to come up with a definitive answer. One thing most of us can agree about is that there is a clear difference between a living body and a dead body, but what is that difference? We know that when a person dies, the body they leave behind is clearly missing the true essence of that person.

Both a living and a recently deceased body are made out of the same material. They both have cells that are still living and functioning. It takes a while after death for the individual cells to stop functioning and die. They both have the same macroscopic and microscopic structure and function. Both the living and the dead are made out of the same molecules and atoms. All those atoms are made out of quantum particles that are made out of nonphysical/spiritual waves. They are both made out of the same stuff operating in the same way in both the physical and nonphysical realms. So, what makes one alive and the other not?

There has to be more to being alive than the material and substance that one is made out of. In other words, the waving spiritual substance that makes up the quantum particles which we (and everything else) are made out of isn't what gives us life and a conscious mind. Dead bodies don't have a conscious mind and can't think anymore. Both things that are living and things that are not are made out of the same spiritual substance. Things that can think and things that can't think are made out of the same spiritual substance.

Therefore, the spiritual substance itself is not responsible for making something alive or for the ability to think.

> *Genesis 2:7 NASB – "Then the LORD God formed man of dust from the ground, and breathed into his nostrils the breath of life; and man became a living being."*
>
> *1 Corinthians 15:45 NASB – "So also it is written, "The first MAN, Adam, BECAME A LIVING SOUL." The last Adam became a life-giving spirit."*

The Scriptures say that God breathed into the first human and gave him the breath of life so that he became a living being or a living soul depending on the translation. It is God who gives life, not the spiritual substance that He created. Also, Jesus, the last Adam, gives us an entirely new level of life in the Spirit. That, however, is another whole book in itself.

Throughout the Scriptures, we see many references to the Spirit of God, angels, demons, and our human spirits. All these types of spiritual beings are recorded in the Bible as being able to talk, think, feel emotions, and make choices. However, we don't see any evidence that the spiritual material that makes up the spirit beings, our spirits, and our bodies has any of these abilities.

However, there are several other religions and belief systems that hold to the belief that the spiritual material itself has a conscious mind. Some proponents of those other belief systems point back to the double slit experiment as proof that there must be some kind of conscious interaction between the observer and the quantum particles. However, we discussed in the last chapter how the double slit experiment can be fully explained without any such metaphysical interaction. The nonphysical wave packets are just acting like wave packets that we have actively changed with our equipment as we measured them. There is nothing in the double slit experiment that indicates that the quantum fields have a mind or a will.

Let's look at another analogy to help us understand the difference more clearly. Clever engineers can take a bunch of metal and silicon and create gears, wires, and microchips. They can then take those components and create a robot that can speak a few words, has artificial intelligence, and can make rudimentary choices. They can also take those same components and make a boat, a clock, or any number of other tools and machines, which don't have artificial intelligence and can't talk or make rudimentary choices. It is up to the designer to decide what to make out of the parts.[1]

It is not the metal itself or the gears and wires that give the robot the potential to have artificial intelligence. The way that the designer puts the pieces together gives the robot that potential. Even the microprocessor itself doesn't give the robot artificial intelligence. The higher intelligence has to program the microprocessor very carefully to give the robot basic artificial intelligence before the potential inherent in the microprocessor becomes reality. The sum of the parts

---

[1] Isaiah 29:16, 45:9-12, 64:8, Jeremiah 18:1-6, Romans 9:20-21

becomes more than the parts when an intelligent designer gets involved.

A large variety of things can be made out of the same basic parts, and each one can have a different level of abilities and "intelligence." The same is true for the quantum particles that make up the universe. The Creator made all kinds of different things out of the same components, all with different abilities, characteristics, and levels of intelligence.

It is not the spiritual stuff we are made out of that makes us a living spirit. It is the way that the Creator designed us and put us together that makes us a living spirit. Everything is made out of a waving spiritual substance, but not everything is alive. Everything is made out of spiritual stuff, but not everything has a living spirit.

There are several other religions and world-views that believe that since everything is made out of spiritual material, since God is Spirit, and since we have a spirit, therefore they must all be the same thing. Thus, they believe that we are all "god" and that the universe itself is "god." This belief misses the distinction between the Creator and the created.

We know that God is omnipresent; He is everywhere and every-when both inside and outside the universe. God created everything that exists. God is holding and sustaining the entire universe and everything in it. Everything that exists is contained within God. We can't get outside of Him. No part of the universe could possibly be outside of God. There is no such thing as outside of God. He is everywhere.

There is nowhere in the universe we can go where we can get away from God (Psalm 139:7-12).[2] Everything is being constantly sustained by God in the deepest smallest parts. God is in everything, but everything is not God. We are not God. The universe is not God. The created isn't the Creator. We need to be careful to maintain that distinction.

The belief that everything spiritual is the same can lead us to believe that each one of us is a god, which is very appealing to our self-centered rebellious nature. The original sin for both Satan and the first humans was trying to be their own god and do things their own way. Every one of us struggles with that temptation to one degree or another at some point in our lives, but we make terrible gods.

We are not smart enough or good enough or loving enough or powerful enough and we have such a limited understanding of what is going on in our own lives, let alone anyone else's, that we do a terrible job at being in charge. A person, a spirit being, or the spiritual realm itself, is much too limited to be a god. It is best to let God be God. He is smart enough, good enough, loving enough, and powerful enough to be sovereign.

---

[2] Although Hell is a region that is "separated from God" according to Christian theology, God still keeps His covenant of love and His covenant with nature and must continue to sustain the existence of those in Hell. Otherwise, they would cease to exist, rather than existing eternally in Hell. God is everywhere. There is nowhere to go that is outside of God. (Psalm 139:8) However, He is not actively in relationship with everyone where everyone can enjoy His goodness and His Lordship. God separates His manifest presence from those in Hell because they have chosen to be separate, but He still maintains their existence.

The belief that all spiritual stuff is the same and therefore it is deity also says that the sum of the parts can't be more than the components regardless of the design. It elevates the metal and plastic over the clever design and programming of the robot in our previous analogy. It ascribes deity to created stuff. It would be like the artificial intelligence in the robot deciding that the metal and plastic it is made out of are its god, rather than the person who made it out of those things.

It also turns their god into an impersonal force that doesn't love, have intelligence, or have a personality, but somehow still has a will. The electromagnetic field, the gravity field, and the other quantum fields don't have a will and they are not deity. The quantum force fields are much too little to be deity. They are just a thing.

When people talk about "spiritual forces talking" to them, they probably don't understand what they are saying. They are actually saying quantum forces like the electromagnetic force or the gravity force was "talking" to them. Does that make sense? No, but when people slap the "spiritual" label on something, suddenly people get all confused and don't know what makes sense and what doesn't. Let's take the mystery out of the spiritual. The spiritual forces are the quantum forces, plain and simple. It is much more likely that their own sub-conscience thoughts, a demon, an angel, or the Holy Spirit was talking to them. It takes intelligence to talk. Spirit beings can talk. Spiritual forces can't.

Our own sub-conscious thoughts and feelings can be very deceptive and so can the demons. Often one or both of these can masquerade as an angel, God, a ghost, or a "spiritual force" in order to get us to agree with what is being said to us. We have to be on our guard and not just believe what the enemy or our own flesh is feeding us.

We also don't always need to blame a demon. Many times, it is our own hearts that are leading us astray. We want to be in charge of our own lives and do things our own way. We want to feel powerful and be in control of what is happening to us. It is base human nature.

We mistakenly believe that we know what is best for us, but we are trapped in our little 4D worlds with our little 4D perspectives. We don't even know what is going on in our own subconscious or in our own circumstances, let alone knowing what is going on with anyone around us. We like to think we understand, but then we realize something about ourselves that we never understood before. We are constantly learning and growing. We can't possibly claim to understand or to know what the best thing to do is. The best we can do is to make an educated guess, which some of us are better at than others, but we are all still just guessing.

God, on the other hand, is not limited in any way. He knows exactly what is going on in the depths of our hearts and in the depths of everyone else's hearts. He knows all of our circumstances and the whole of history past, present, and future. He is powerful and in control of the laws of nature. He is not insecure or afraid like we are. God is good and loving all the time. That is His nature. He can't not be good and loving. God is love. We can trust God and let Him be God.

Also, we can worship God. We automatically give control of our lives over to whatever we worship. Whatever we worship becomes the lord of our lives. When we worship ourselves by trying to be our own gods, we worship something so small and limited. When we worship a spirit being or any created thing, we are worshipping something inherently limited. If we worship the spiritual realm itself, or even worship the whole universe in all its awesomely immense size, grandeur, and mystery, we are still worshipping something created and inherently limited.

Anything inside the universe pales in comparison to the God who created the universe and holds it in His hand. The unimaginably gigantic universe is still tiny compared to God. God is uncreated and unlimited. As for me, I believe that any created thing or even creation itself is too small to be worshipped or to give control of my life over to. Any created thing is far too limited for me to trust to be my Lord. However, God is good and unlimited. He can be fully and completely trusted.

I have heard that sound waves and light waves are the same thing at different frequencies. Is that true?

No, it is not true. Sound and electromagnetic waves, such as light, are very different types of waves. They aren't just waving at different frequencies. In fact, some electromagnetic waves are waving at the same frequencies as audible sound waves.

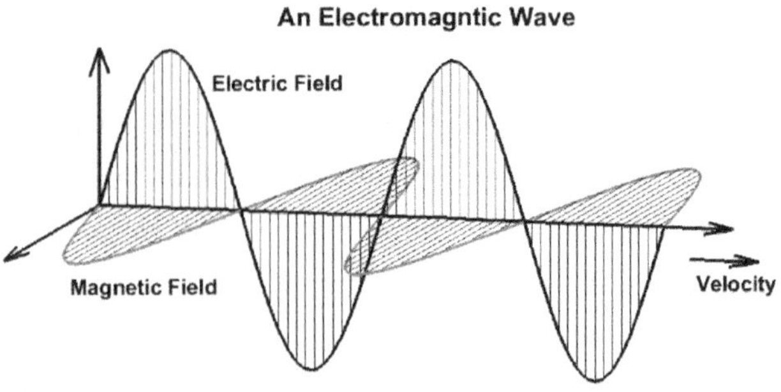

An Electromagntic Wave

Figure 18: An electromagnetic wave. The Electric field vibrates perpendicularly to the magnetic field, which vibrates perpendicularly to the motion of the wave front.

The audible hearing range is about 20 to 20,000Hz. A Hertz is one cycle per second. A wave at 20 Hz oscillates up and down twenty times in one second, and a wave at 20,000 Hz oscillates up and down 20,000 times in one second. The radio wave part of the electromagnetic spectrum ranges from 3 Hz to 3000 GHz (3,000,000,000,000 Hz). Therefore, the range of radio waves completely overlaps the audible hearing range. Radio waves are oscillating at the same frequencies as the audible hearing range, but we can't hear them directly. We have to use a radio to translate the radio waves into sound waves so we can hear them.

Sound waves are physical waves and require physical 3D objects like air or water for the waves to move through. On the other hand, light is a nonphysical wave. It does not need a physical medium to move through. Light and other electromagnetic waves can propagate through the vacuum of empty space. Sound interacts with atoms and bigger objects. Light interacts with electrons as we discussed in the chapter

A) A Transverse Wave

B) A Longitudinal Wave

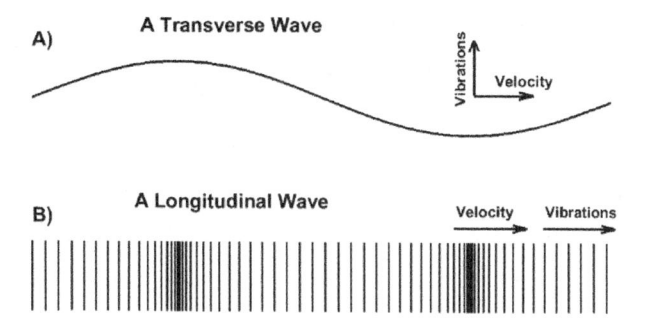

Figure 19: A Transverse wave vibrates perpendicular to the motion of the wave front. A longitudinal wave vibrates in the same direction as the motion of the wave front.

on Quantum Leaping. Sound shakes physical things. Light shakes the nonphysical electromagnetic field.

Electromagnetic waves are transverse waves (see Figure 18). They vibrate the electromagnetic field perpendicularly to the direction the wave front is moving in. The electric wave is perpendicular to the magnetic wave, which is perpendicular to the motion of the wave front. Thus, light needs three directions/dimensions to describe it. Light is multi-dimensional.

Sound is a density wave (see Figure 19), so it makes the air or water or other medium denser in some places and less dense in other places. In other words, the wave is alternately squishing the medium closer together and pulling it farther apart. This type of wave is a longitudinal wave. That means is it vibrating in the same direction that the wave front is moving. Thus, sound is operating in one-dimension.

Sound and light are completely different types of waves. They are both waves with constant frequency and amplitude, like all waves, but all the other characteristics are different.

Speeding up the sound wave won't turn it into a light wave. They are fundamentally different.

When people have visions of heaven or have spiritual experiences in the Bible and in modern times, they often report that the sounds of heaven seem very tightly linked to the light in heaven. Therefore, many people have assumed that the heavenly sounds are the same as the heavenly light, but this is an overly simplistic assumption. Sound and light are totally different types of waves. Sound is a physical wave and heaven is an entirely nonphysical realm, so what is the "sound" in heaven?

Recall from our discussion on optical illusions that the brain will automatically pick the closest past experience that it can to the present experience and frame the current experience in terms of the previous experience. Most of us have a large library of sights, sounds, and scents to pull from, but we have a small library of spiritual sensory data to pull from. When a person has a spiritual experience or a heavenly experience, the brain interprets all the spiritual sensory data in terms of physical sensory data. Thus, the person experiences familiar sights, sounds, and scents as a way to make sense out of the spiritual experience.

We always have to remember that the way our brains perceive events is not the absolute reality of the event itself. Everyone perceives every experience through the filter of his or her past experiences. It is the same with spiritual experiences. We all interpret the nonphysical data in terms of our physical senses. All the spiritual sensory data is nonphysical and coming in through our spirits, so it always feels like it is one thing. No matter how our brains choose to interpret the nonphysical data as sounds, light, scents, taste, or touch it all comes from the same source, so it all seems integrated. Heavenly spiritual things are naturally much more integrated and unified than physical things as well. The fact that sound and light seem like the same thing in many heavenly experiences is more a reflection of how the brain processes data, rather than saying anything about "heavenly sound" and light itself.

Different people process sensory data differently. Some people are auditory learners and others are visual learners, while still others are kinetic/movement learners. There are different parts of the brain that dominate how each person processes the sensory input from the world around them. Everyone has a unique makeup in the way his or her brain uniquely processes sensory and other information. Someone who is an auditory learner will be much more likely to perceive spiritual experiences in terms of sounds, while a visual learner will perceive the same spiritual experience in terms of sights. The spiritual data didn't change, but the two different brains processed and reported the information differently.

We should look for the similarities across the gamut of spiritual experiences that we hear about, rather than nit-picking about the differences. The things that are constant across many people's perceptions are more likely to point to something real, rather than just pointing to the way that humans perceive the nonphysical higher dimensional realm. We also have to translate back to the nonphysical data from the 4D boxes that all our brains automatically put the data in before we could comprehend it ourselves or describe it to someone else.

We also need to remember that God will show each one of us what we need to see and hear in each moment to help us along on our unique journey. What we need to see and hear from God at one point in our journey will be very different from what we need to know in another point in our journey. Also, what someone else needs to experience to learn the next lesson is different from what we need to experience to learn our next lesson. Thus, everyone will have different spiritual experiences from God based on where they are at and what they need right then.

We need to be humble about putting too much stock in the way that our brains process spiritual or physical data and keep in close communication with the Holy Spirit who knows what reality actually is. Our perceptions are always inaccurate, but we can know what is actually going on if we ask God. The Holy Spirit will guide us into all truth, that is His job and He is good at it.

> *John 16:13, "But when he, the Spirit of truth, comes, he will guide you into all the truth. He will not speak on his own; he will speak only what he hears, and he will tell you what is yet to come."*

Chapter 8
Conclusion

We have discovered that everything physical is made out of nonphysical waves and interacts through nonphysical forces. We are all made out of fuzzy balls of waving nonphysical/spiritual stuff that is confined to a three-dimensional shape, and thus appears to be physical. All the interactions between the fuzzy balls of spiritual stuff also occur though nonphysical/spiritual forces. Therefore, everything is fundamentally spiritual. Even our physical bodies and physical touch are fundamentally spiritual. We are spiritual beings living in a spiritual world.

We have discovered that Someone (or something) is waving nothing and making something. Now, you can choose to believe that the universe and all of us are made out of random waves of nothing or you can choose to believe that we are all made out of something nonphysical which Someone or something is waving. I personally believe that the God of the Bible is that Someone who is waving some created spiritual substance and thus making us and the whole universe exist. God loves us and wants to be with us, so He created us, and He created the universe for us to live in.

The Bible says that God is holding the whole universe in His hand.[1] The physical part of the universe is at least 78 billion light years across in each direction, but the nonphysical, unseen, spiritual part of the universe is unimaginably bigger. That certainly puts our circumstances and troubles into perspective doesn't it?

God is intimately holding the entire universe and each of us in the depths of our nonphysical waves. God is holding our physical bodies and our circumstances together, and He is holding our spirits and souls together. God is holding us from the innermost part of our being all the way out to every part of our whole bodies. He is sustaining us in every moment of our existence both inside time and beyond time. God is in the tiniest detail and beyond the highest heavens.

We can choose to focus on our "light and momentary troubles"[2] and ignore God's love, presence, power, and brilliance. We can choose to go our own way and try to fix all of our problems by ourselves, or we can choose to focus on how God is always intimately present right where we are and focus on how God lovingly wants to help us with His power and His brilliance. God has brilliant solutions for every circumstance that we face. God is so much bigger and more powerful than our problems.

---

[1] Psalms 95:3-5, 102:25-27, Job 38:4-5, Isaiah 40:10-15
[2] 2 Corinthians 4:17

Not only is God sustaining the whole universe and every quantum particle, He is also completely in control of all the laws of nature. He can and does do miracles on our behalf regularly. Some of the miracles are big and obvious, but many are little and seemingly ordinary. God is always working and helping us in the little everyday things and in the bigger crises we occasionally face.

We have seen how flexible God made the laws of nature so that He can do any miracle He wants without violating any of the rules. God can use quantum leaping and tunneling to move particles around, or He can use any other method He likes. There is nothing that is impossible, or even difficult, for God. Our problems and needs are not too difficult for Him to help us with.

He also gave us the ability use the laws of nature to make technology and medicine to benefit each other. We discovered that God gave us so many abilities in the unseen realm that we have only just begun to tap into. For example, the concept of quantum tunneling allows things to go where they are normally forbidden to go. Quantum leaping makes things pop out of the physical realm and pop back in somewhere else by becoming entirely nonphysical for a moment. There are so many abilities hidden within the physics of the universe. We are still just babies in our ability to tap into these inherent abilities, but God is more than capable of using these innate abilities to bring good gifts to His children.

As we trust in God and learn from Him, we can let go of our own trust and dependence on the limited physical realm, and we can let ourselves learn and grow in our natural spiritual abilities. We have learned so much, but there is still so much yet to learn. There is no end to our ability to learn, grow, and deepen our understanding of who God is, how God made us, and how the spiritual realm works. All we have to do is maintain humility and a teachable heart.

When we ask God for help, He gives us solutions that take us past seemingly impossible obstacles and into new places that we never dreamed possible. As we keep our eyes on the reality of Heaven and the reality of who God is, the physical constraints of our circumstances lose their grip on us. Then, we can move into more of the freedom God gives us in the spiritual realm to become more like Him.

> *2 Corinthians 5:16, "So from now on we regard no one from a worldly point of view. Though we once regarded Christ in this way, we do so no longer."*

As we turn away from our worldly point of view, we can see more and more from a spiritual point of view and see others, our circumstances, and ourselves in the way that Christ sees them, which is true reality. When we trust God's perception of reality above our own views, our thinking becomes less limited and we see solutions to our problems and paths around obstacles that we couldn't see before. God's ways are higher than our ways. He has solutions we couldn't even dream of, and He will freely engage with us to put those solutions into effect in our lives as we cooperate with Him.

We also discussed the concept of superfluids, superconductors, and BECs, where all the quantum particles come into complete unity with each other. In this state, all the nonphysical/spiritual abilities of each individual member of the group are aligned with all the others and magnified for all to see. In this unified state, the whole group can manifest their innate nonphysical/spiritual abilities and do things that look like super powers such as: moving with no resistance, being able to escape from the tightest confinement, doing things without losing energy, and being at rest regardless of the circumstances.

There is no competition or conflict within the group. Every member is doing its part to contribute to the whole. God wants all His children to come into complete unity with Himself and with each other. We can't get there with our own strength and ideas. Only God can bring human beings into unity with each other. His desire is for His love and unity to flow into us and through us without any hindrances. God is working on bringing all of us into true love and true unity. We can let go of going our own way, and we can trust Him in the process.

God is not far away in Heaven, disconnected or disinterested. The heavenly realm is perpendicular to the physical realm, intersecting with us right now, everywhere and every-when. It is not far away or hard to reach. Through the Holy Spirit living in us, we have full access to the heavenly realm, right here and now. The Holy Spirit is a great teacher, and He shows us how to become more Christ-like in our thinking, feelings, and behavior.

If someone hasn't asked Christ to come into his or her heart yet, there is no better time than now to do so. God is already intimately holding each person whether they are a Christian or not, but He also wants to have a relationship with each person and talk to us and help us. God wants us to know Him as much as He already knows everything about us. God wants His love to flow into our hearts and build relationship with us.

God loves us no matter what we have done or ever will do. It is no surprise to God. He had already seen the whole movie before He decided to create us, and He created us anyway! That is how much God loves us. No matter how much we and everyone else have screwed up, God still wants to be in a relationship with us forever. God knows all about our weaknesses and problems, but God also knows how powerful He is to save us from our issues and problems. It's about His power not ours.

God knows all about our past and future choices whether good or bad, but He also knows what we are like in our eternal state: the best version of ourselves or the worst version of ourselves. God looks at the heart, not the outward appearance.[3] It is up to us to choose to let God draw us into our heavenly best eternal state or to let the enemy draw us into some other eternal state.

If you haven't let Jesus come into your heart and start transforming you into the best version of yourself, I encourage you to do so. If you have let Jesus into your heart, I encourage you to pray for an ever-deepening revelation of

---

[3] 1 Samuel 16:7

God's nearness, love, and power. I encourage you to continue to partner with God on your journey to becoming the best version of yourself.

We can ask God to give us a greater revelation of our true identity in Christ as He lovingly designed us to be in eternity. We can work together with the Holy Spirit to align our thoughts, emotions, speech, and actions with that reality more and more. We can invite the Holy Spirit to guide us into all truth and to help us understand the Word of God in all its full higher dimensional, nonphysical truth. We can invite the Holy Spirit to teach us to access the fullness of how God created each of us to be in spirit, soul, and body, and in relationship with Him. We can work together with God to come into His true love and unity with the whole Body of Christ and with the Head, Jesus. We can have confidence that God will answer our prayers and help us because He wants us to have all of these things.

> *1 John 5:14-15, "This is the confidence we have in approaching God: that if we ask anything according to his will, he hears us. And if we know that he hears us--whatever we ask--we know that we have what we asked of him."*

About the Author

Dr. Sarah McGee received her Ph.D. in Theoretical Quantum Physics from the University of Colorado in 2012. She grew up in a family that was deeply involved with doing homeless ministry and frequently saw the Lord do many miracles. Her family also had a deep respect and love for theology and science. This gave Sarah a deep appreciation for the Creator and the creation. She has a great desire to see the areas of theology and science reconciled by the love of the One who made them both. Sarah is the founder of the ministry, Jesus Reigns Eternal. (JesusReignsEternal.org)